A BILINGUAL INDEX

OF

NYĀYA-BINDU

न्यायबिन्दु

A BILINGUAL INDEX

OF

NYĀYA-BINDU

न्यायबिन्दु

BY

SIR WILLIAM JONES

EDITOR

SATIS CHANDRA VIDYABHUSANA

GYAN

Published by

Gyan Publishing House
5, Ansari Road
Daryaganj, New Delhi-110002
Phone: 011-47034999, 9811692060
E-mail: books@gyanbooks.com

Distribution Network
gyanbooks.com
India, USA, Canada, UK, Australia

ISBN: 978-93-6433-196-8 (PB)
First Published, 1917

2nd Impression 2024

Printed at: Gyan Press, Delhi.

A BILINGUAL INDEX OF NYĀYA-BINDU
Author: SIR WILLIAM JONES
Editor: SATIS CHANDRA VIDYABHUSANA

BIBLIOTHECA INDICA:
A
COLLECTION OF ORIENTAL WORKS
PUBLISHED BY THE
ASIATIC SOCIETY OF BENGAL.
New Series, No. 1408.

A BILINGUAL INDEX
OF
NYĀYA-BINDU.

न्यायबिन्दु ।

རིགས་པའི་ཐིགས་པ།

PREPARED AND EDITED BY
MAHAMAHOPADHYAYA SATIS CHANDRA VIDYABHUSANA, M.A., Ph.D., M.R.A.S., F.A.S.B.
Principal, Sanskrit College, Calcutta; Jt. Philological Secretary, Asiatic Society of Bengal; and Fellow of the Calcutta University.

CALCUTTA:
PRINTED AT THE BAPTIST MISSION PRESS,
AND PUBLISHED BY THE
ASIATIC SOCIETY, 1, PARK STREET,
1917.

PREFACE.

The present volume contains an Index of Sanskrit and Tibetan words occurring in the original text of the Nyāya-bindu and its Tibetan version respectively. To enable scholars to interpret accurately the technical philosophical words in Sanskrit and Tibetan, I have taken great pains to show the mutual correspondence between words of the two languages as used in the two texts of the Nyāya-bindu.

The Nyāya-bindu was a stranger to Brāhmaṇic India until it was discovered among the palm-leaf manuscripts preserved in the Jaina temple of Śāntinātha, Cambay, and published in the Bibliotheca Indica series of Calcutta under the editorship of Professor P. Peterson in A.D. 1889. The Tibetan version which existed in the Tangyur (Mdo, Ce, leaves 347-355) has been published in the Bibliotheca Buddhica series of St. Petersburgh (Petrograd) under the editorship of Professor F. J. Sherbatski. The Index presented herewith is based upon the Sanskrit text of the Nyāya-bindu as edited by Professor Peterson as also on the Tibetan version as edited by Professor Sherbatski.

Professor Peterson has also edited a Sanskrit commentary on the Nyāya-bindu called Nyāya-bindu-ṭīkā by Dharmottarācāryya, while Professor Sherbatski has edited the Tibetan version of it. A bilingual Index of this commentary is under preparation.

Another edition of the Tibetan version of the Nyāya-bindu together with the commentary of Vinīta-deva has lately been published in the Bibliotheca Indica series of Calcutta under the editorship of Professor Louis De La Vallee Poussin of Ghent, Belgium. While engaged in preparing my Index I was informed that Professor Sherbatski was publishing a new edition of the Sanskrit Nyāya-bindu. During his visit to Calcutta in 1911, the Professor very kindly asked me to publish my Index of the Nyāya-bindu in the Bibliotheca Buddhica series of St. Petersburgh When I was expecting Professor Sherbatski's Sanskrit edition and making arrangements for sending the copy of my Index to St. Petersburgh, the great European War broke out on the 1st August 1914, and I was obliged to abandon the project of having my work published in the Bibliotheca Buddhica series. The Council of the Asiatic Society of Bengal having kindly agreed to include my aforesaid Index in the Bibliotheca Indica series, I bring out the present edition without further delay.

SANSKRIT COLLEGE, CALCUTTA.
The 15th October, 1916. } SATIS CHANDRA VIDYABHUSANA.

INTRODUCTION.

The Nyāya-bindu, called in Tibetan Rigs-paḫi-thigs-pa, is a most abstruse work on Buddhist Logic. It is divided into three chapters dealing respectively with (1) perception (प्रत्यक्ष མངོན་སུམ), (2) inference for one's self (स्वार्थानुमान བདག་གི་དོན་གྱི་རྗེས་སུ་དཔག་པ) and (3) inference for the sake of others (परार्थानुमान གཞན་གྱི་དོན་རྗེས་སུ་དཔག་པ)।

Nyāya-bindu.

The Nyāya-bindu is a work of Dharmakīrti (ཆོས་གྲགས) who, besides this work, wrote a number of excellent treatises on Logic such as Pramāṇa-vārtika-kārikā, Pramāṇa-vārtika-vṛtti, Pramāṇa-viniścaya, Hetubindu-vivaraṇa, Vāda-nyāya (or Tarka-nyāya), Santānāntara-siddhi, Sambandha-parīkṣā and Sambandha-parīkṣā-vṛtti. None of these treatises is now available in Sanskrit but the Tibetan versions of all of them are preserved in the Tangyur, Mdo, Ce.

The colophon to the Pramāṇa-vārtika-kārikā runs as follows:—

ཚད་མ་རྣམས་འགྲེལ་ཚིག་ལེའུར་བྱས་པ།
ཡུལ་ལྷོ་ཕྱོགས་ཀྱི་རྒྱུད་དུ་བྱུང་བ།
གཞུང་ལུགས་ངན་པ་ཐམས་ཅད་ཆེས་ཤིན་དུ་འཁྲུལ་པར་འཇུག་པ།
སྙན་པའི་གྲགས་པས་སའི་སྟེང་མ་ལུས་པ་ཁྱབ་པ།
འགྲན་ཟླ་མེད་པའི་མཁས་པ་ཆེན་པོ་དཔལ་ཆོས་ཀྱི་གྲགས་པས་མཛད་པ་རྫོགས་སོ།།

(Tangyur, Mdo, Ce, leaf 258).

"Here is finished the Pramāṇavārtika-kārikā which is a work of Śrī Dharmakīrti who was born in a family of the Deccan, who exposed largely the errors of all the vicious texts (of the Tīrthikas), whose fame filled the entire earth and who as a great sage had no rival."

Life of Dharma-kīrti.

Lama Tārānātha, in his History of Indian Buddhism called "Chos-byuṅ,"[1] says that Dharmakīrti, according to all accounts of earlier sages, was born in the south in the kingdom of Cūḍāmaṇi which he identifies with Trimalaya. Dharmakīrti, whose father was a Tīrthika of the Brāhmaṇa caste, was well versed in the Vedas, Vedāṅgas, art of healing, etc. By occasionally attending lectures of the Buddhist preachers, he was so much impressed with the purity of Buddhism that he became a convert to it. He came to Magadha where he was received into the fraternity of Ācāryya Dharmapāla. Gradually he attained to great proficiency in the three Piṭakas and knew in all 500 sūtras and dhāraṇīs by heart.

Dharmakīrti and Kumārila.

According to some Tibetan authorities Dharmakīrti was a nephew of Kumārila Bhaṭṭa the great philosopher of the Mīmāṁsā school. Though Tārānātha does not attach much value to this tradition, he affirms that Dharmakīrti lived in disguise for a long time with Kumārila from whom he acquired all the secret doctrines of the Brāhmaṇas. Tradition goes so far as to say that Kumārila, being defeated by Dharmakīrti in a debate, adopted the Buddhistic faith at the last stage of his life. This tradition is recorded not only in the "Chos-byuṅ" but is repeated also in the Ḏpag-ḇsam-ḻjon-ḇzaṅ" as follows:—

དེའི་ཚེ་གཞོན་ནུ་རོལ་པས་ཁྲོས་ནས་ཁྲིམས་ཏེ་འཁོར་ལྔ་བརྒྱ་བཅས་འོང་
ནས་བརྩོས་ཚེ་ཁོ་བོ་འི་ཐུན་མོང་མིན་པའི་དམ་བཅས་ལྔ་བརྒྱ་པོ་སྲུན་ཕྱུང་སྟེ་ནང་
པར་གཞུགས།

(Ḏpag-ḇsam-ḻjon-ḇzaṅ, edited by Sarat Chandra Das, p. 106).

"Upon this Kumārila was enraged and appeared with 500 attendants for debate. Being defeated he with his attendants became, in pursuance of his extraordinary pledge, followers of Buddha."

[1] Lama Tārānātha's Geschichte des Buddhismus von Schiefner, pp. 175-185.

Dharmakīrti further withstood the Nirgranthas, Rāhuvratin and others, who lived within the range of the Vindhya mountains. While sojourning there he was invited by a neighbouring king who as a token of honour had the following inscription recorded at his gate:—

Dharmakīrti's triumph.

གལ་ཏེ་ཆོས་ཀྱི་གྲགས་པ་ཡི།

སྨྲ་བའི་ཉི་མ་ནུབ་པ་ན།

ཆོས་རྣམས་གཉིད་ལོག་ཡང་ན་ཤི།

ཆོས་མ་ཡིན་རྣམས་ད་གདོད་ལོངས།།

(D̲pag-b̲sam-l̲jon-b̲zaṅ, p. 106).

"If Dharmakīrti, the sun among disputants, sets and his doctrines sleep or die, the false doctrines of the Tīrthikas will then rise."

Returning to the south Dharmakīrti challenged by criers those who were ready for debate. The majority of the Tīrthikas fled; and some actually confessed that they were not equal to the fight. After defeating all his rivals in the Deccan and some parts of Northern India, he, towards the end of his life, built a monastery in the land of Kaliṅga where he died.

Dharmakīrti was a contemporary of the Tibetan King Sroṅ-b̲tsan-s̲gam-po, and must therefore have lived early in the 7th century A.D. This is borne out by the fact that he was a pupil of Dharmapāla who retired from the university of Nālandā by A.D. 635, when Śīlabhadra was at the head of the university. Hwen-thsang, who visited Kauśāmbī in December, A.D. 636, found there the ruins of a monastery where Dharmapāla had refuted the arguments of the heretics. It seems that in A.D. 635 Dharmakīrti was very young as Hwen-thsang does not mention him. On the other hand Itsing, who travelled over India during A.D. 671-695, declares eloquently how Dharmakīrti "made further development in Logic after Dignāga."[1]

Age of Dharmakīrti.

---

[1] "I-tsing" translated by Takakusu, p. lviii.

Dharmakīrti opposes Dignāga.

Dharmakīrti, whose avowed intention was to support Dignāga, did not sometimes refrain from opposing him. Dignāga in his Nyāya-praveśa[1] mentions a fallacy called the "contradiction of the middle term to the *real* major term" (स्वभावविरुद्ध ཆོས་ཀྱི་རང་བཞིན་ཕྱིན་ཅི་ལོག་ཏུ་སྒྲུབ་པར་བྱེད་པ) and another called the "contradiction of the middle term to the *implied* major term" (इष्ट-विघातकृद्विरुद्ध ཆོས་ཀྱི་ཁྱད་པར་ཕྱིན་ཅི་ལོག་ཏུ་སྒྲུབ་པར་བྱེད་པ)।

The first fallacy is illustrated as follows:—

Contradiction of the middle term to the real major term.

Sound is eternal,
Because it is a product of effort.

Here there is contradiction between "product of effort" which is the middle term and "eternal" which is the real major term, and therefore the reasoning is fallacious.

An illustration of the second fallacy is given below:—

Contradiction of the middle term to the implied major term.

The eyes etc. are for the use of another,
Because they are composite things,
Like a bed, seat, etc.

Here the major term "another" is ambiguous in as much as it may signify either a composite thing (e.g. the body) or a non composite thing (e.g. the soul). There would be a contradiction between the middle term and the major term if the word "another" were used by the speaker in the sense of a non-composite thing, but understood by the listener in the sense of a composite thing. This reasoning which involves a "contradiction of the middle term to the desired or implied major term," is fallacious.

Dharmakīrti in his Nyāyā-bindu[2] does not recognize this second fallacy in as much as it is, in his opinion, included in the first. A word, which is the major term of a proposition, can as such admit of only one meaning, and if there is ambiguity between the meaning expressed and the meaning implied the real meaning is to be ascertained from the context.[2]

---

[1] Tangyur, Mdo, Ce, leaf 186.

[2] Nyāya-bindu, A.S.B., Chap. III, pp. 113-114.

Dignāga[1] mentions yet another fallacy called the "non-erratic contradiction" (विरुद्धाव्यभिचारी འགལ་བ་ལ་མི་འཁྲུལ་བ) which he includes among the "fallacies of uncertainty." It takes place when two contradictory conclusions are supported by what appear to be valid reasons, e.g.

Non-erratic contradiction.

A Vaiśeṣika philosopher says:—

> Sound is non-eternal,
> Because it is a product.

A Mīmāṁsaka replies:—

> Sound is eternal,
> Because it is audible.

The reasons employed in the above cases are supposed both to be correct according, respectively, to the tenets of the Vaiśeṣika and Mīmāṁsā schools, but as they lead to contradictory conclusions they are uncertain and as such fallacious.

Dharmakīrti in the Nyāya-bindu[2] rejects this fallacy of "non-erratic contradiction," on the ground that it does not arise in connection with inference and is not based even on the scripture. A reason or middle term, which is valid, must stand to the major term in the relation of identity, causality or non-perception, and must lead to correct conclusion. Two conclusions which are contradictory cannot therefore be supported by reasons which are valid. Two different sets of scripture too cannot be of any help in the establishment of two contradictory conclusions inasmuch as a scripture cannot override perception and inference, and is authoritative only in the ascertainment of supersensuous objects. The non-erratic contradiction is therefore impossible.

Uddyotakara, a Brāhmaṇic logician and author of the Nyāya-vārtika, quotes Dharmakīrti's definition of a proposition (प्रतिज्ञा དམ་བཅའ) from the Vāda-vidhi[3] (same as Vāda-nyāya) and discusses at length the Bud-

Dharmakīrti and Uddyotakara criticise each other.

---

[1] Nyāya-praveśa in the Tangyur, Mdo, Ce, leaf 185.

[2] Nyāya-bindu, Chap. III, p. 115.

[3] यदपि वादविधौ साध्याभिधानं प्रतिज्ञेति प्रतिज्ञालक्षणमुक्तम् । (Nyāya-vartika, 1-33, p. 121, A.S.B.).

དམ་བཅའ་བ་ཡང་བསྒྲུབ་བྱ་བརྗོད་པའི་ཕྱིར་རོ། (Vāda-nyāya in the Tangyur, Mdo, Ce, leaf 399).

dhist definition[1] of *sādhya* (major term). Dharmakīrti in the Nyāya-bindu defends his own position against the attack of Uddyotakara who is designated as a S'āstrakāra.[2] There is no doubt that Uddyotakara and Dharmakīrti were contemporaries and that the Vāda-nyāya preceded the Nyāya-vārtika which was followed by the Nyāya-bindu.

SANSKRIT COLLEGE, CALCUTTA.
The 15*th October*, 1916.

SATIS CHANDRA VIDYABHUSANA.

---

1 Nyāvartika, 1-33, pp. 116-121, A.S.B.

Dignāga defines a "sādhya" or "anumeya" as follows :—

स्वरूपेणैव निर्देश्यः
स्वयमिष्टः स्वधर्मिणि ।
प्रत्यक्षार्थानुमानेन
चाप्तवाचाऽनिराकृतः ॥

(Pramāṇa-samuccaya, Chap. III).

The above Sanskrit śloka is the retranslation of the following verse of the Tibetan version :—

རང་གི་ངོ་བོ་ཁོ་ན་བསྟན
བདག་འདོད་རང་གི་ཆོས་ཅན་ལ །
མངོན་སུམ་དོན་དང་རྗེས་དཔག་དང་
ཡིད་ཆེས་གྲགས་པས་མ་བསལ་བའོ ॥

(Pramāṇa-samuccaya, Chap. III, in Tangyur, Mdo, Ce, pp. 1-13).

2 Nyāya-bindu, Chap. III, pp. 110-111.

A BILINGUAL INDEX OF NYĀYA-BINDU.

SANSKRIT WORDS WITH TIBETAN EQUIVALENTS.

अ ।

अ	११५	མ
अज्ञातक	११८	མ་གྲགས་པ
अग्नि	१०४, १०६, १०९, ११२, ११६	མེ
अग्नेः	१०५, १०६	མེ་ཡོད་པའི་ཕྱིར
अङ्ग	१११	ཡན་ལག
अङ्गवत्	११३	ཡན་ལག་བཞིན་ནོ
अचन्द्र	१११	ཟླ་བ་མ་ཡིན་ནོ
अचेतनाः	११२	སེམས་པ་མེད་པར
अत एव	११४	དེ་ཉིད་ཀྱི་ཕྱིར
अतत्स्वभावस्य	१०५	དེའི་རང་བཞིན་མ་ཡིན་པ
अतदुत्पत्तेः	१०५	བྱུང་བ་མ་ཡིན་པ་ནི
अतिशय	११७	ཕུལ་དུ་ཕྱིན་པ
अतीत	१०५	འདས་པ
अत्र	१०४, १११, ११७	འདིར
अत्र	१०५, १०६, ११०	འདི་ན
अत्र	१०९	འདི་ན་ནི

Sanskrit	Page	Tibetan
अत्र ...	... १०४ ...	... འདི་ལ
अत्र ...	... ११४ ...	... འདི་ལ་ནི
अत्र ...	... १०४ ...	... དེ་ན
अदर्शन ...	... ११३ ...	... མ་མཐོང་དུ་ཟིན
अदृश्य ...	... ११३ ...	... བལྟར་མི་སྣང་བ
अधिकरणत्वात्	... १११ ...	... གཞི་ཡིན་པའི་ཕྱིར་རོ
अनन्तर ...	... १०३ ...	... མ་ཐག་པ
अनन्तर ...	... १०३ ...	... དེ་མ་ཐག་པ
अनन्तरीयकत्व	... ११३ ...	... མ་ཐག་ཏུ་བྱུང་བ་ཉིད
अनन्वय ...	... ११६ ...	... རྗེས་སུ་འགྲོ་བ་མེད་པ
अनयोः ...	... ११० ...	... འདི (gen.)
अनयोः ...	... १०८ ...	... འདི་གཉིས (gen.)
अनयोः ...	... ११३ ...	... འདི་གཉིས་ནི (gen.)
अनयोः ...	... ११४ ...	... འདི་གཉིས་ལས
अनयोरेव ...	... ११३ ...	... འདི་གཉིས་ཁོ་ནའི
अनात्मक ...	... ११४ ...	... བདག་མེད་པ
अनाप्त ...	... ११७ ...	... ཡིད་ཆེས་པ་མ
अनाप्तता ...	... ११७ ...	... ཡིད་ཆེས་པ་མ་ཡིན་པ
अनाहित ...	... १०३ ...	... མ་སྐྱེད་པའི
अनित्य ...	... ११२, ११६, ११८	མི་རྟག་པ
अनित्य ...	... १०८ ...	... མི་རྟག་པའོ
अनित्य ...	... १०८ ...	... མི་རྟག་པ་སྟེ

अनित्यत्व ...	... १०९, ११६ ...	མི་རྟག་པ་ཉིད
अनित्यत्व ...	... ११२	མི་རྟག་པ་ཉིད་ནི
अनित्यत्वे ...	... ११०	མི་རྟག་པ་ཉིད་དུ
अनिराकृत	... १११	མ་བསལ་བ
अनिराकृत	... ११०	མ་བསལ་བས
अनिराकृत	... १११	མ་བསལ་བ་ནི
अनिष्ट ...	... १११	མི་འདོད་པ
अनिष्पन्नस्य	... १०८	མ་གྲུབ་ན
अनुक्त ...	... १११	མ་སྨྲས
अनुक्ति ...	... १११	མ་བརྗོད
अनुक्तौ ...	... १११	མ་སྨྲས་ན
अनुपलब्धि	... ११३	མི་དམིགས
अनुपलब्धि	... १०४, १०५, १०६, १०७, १०९	མི་དམིགས་པ
अनुपलब्धि	... १०४, १०५, १०६	མི་དམིགས་པ་ནི
अनुपलब्धिलक्षणप्राप्तेषु	१०५	དོན་དམིགས་པའི་རིག་བྱར་མ་གྱུར་པ་རྣམས་ལ
अनुपलब्धेः	... १०४, १०५ ...	མི་དམིགས་པའི་ཕྱིར་རོ
अनुपलब्धौ	... ११०	མི་དམིགས་པ་ལ
अनुपलब्धौ	... १०६	མི་དམིགས་པའི་ནང་དུ
अनुपलब्ध्या	... १०७	མི་དམིགས་པས
अनुपलभ्यमान	... ११०	མི་དམིགས་ན

Sanskrit	Pages	Tibetan
अनुपलब्ध	११५	མི་དམིགས་པ
अनुपलम्भस्य	११२	མི་དམིགས་པའི
अनुपलम्भेषु	११५	མི་དམིགས་པ་དག་ལ
अनुबन्ध	११६	རྗེས་སུ་འཇུག་པ
अनुबन्धिनी	११५	རྗེས་སུ་འཇུག་པའི
अनुबन्धे	१०८	རྗེས་སུ་འབྲེལ་པར
अनुमान	१०३, १०७, १११, ११५	རྗེས་སུ་དཔག་པ
अनुमान	१११	རྗེས་སུ་དཔག་པས
अनुमान	१०४, १११	རྗེས་སུ་དཔག་པ་ནི
अनुमाने	१०६	རྗེས་སུ་དཔག་པ་ལ
अनुमेय	१०४	རྗེས་སུ་དཔག་པར་བྱ་བ
अनुमेय	१०४	རྗེས་སུ་དཔག་པར་བྱ་བ་ནི
अनेक	११०	མང་ཞིག
अनेन	१११	དེས་ན
अनेन	११२	དེ་ནི (instr.)
अनैकान्तिक	११२, ११३, ११४	མ་ངེས་པ
अनैकान्तिकाः	११५	མ་ངེས་པ་དག
अन्तर	१०४, १०६	གཞན
अन्तरालेषु	११५	བར་རྣམས་ལ
अन्तर्भावात्	११३	ནང་དུ་འདུས་པའི་ཕྱིར་རོ
अन्य	१०४, १०८	གཞན

अन्य	१०४	གཞན་པ
अन्य	१०३, ११४, ११५	གཞན་ནི
अन्यत्र	१०८	མ་གཏོགས་པར
अन्यथा	१०५, ११६	གཞན་དུ་ན
अन्यभाव	११३	གཞན་ཡོད་ན
अन्येषाम्	१०७	གཞན་དག་ལ་ནི
अन्योन्य	११४	ཕན་ཚུན
अन्वय	१०९, ११०, ११४, ११६	རྗེས་སུ་འགྲོ་བ
अन्वयमुख	१०९	རྗེས་སུ་འགྲོ་བའི་སྒོ
अन्वेति	११४	རྗེས་སུ་འགྲོ་བ
अपर	११४	ཅིག་ཤོས
अपरस्य	१०९	གཞན (gen.)
अपरस्य	११४	ཅིག་ཤོས་ལ་ནི
अपहरणे	११२	བཀྲུས་ན
अपि	१०४, १०५, १०६, १०९, ११०, १११, ११२, ११३, ११४, ११५	ཡང་
अपि	१०६, १०७, १०९, ११०, १११, ११३, ११६, ११७	ཀྱང་
अपेक्षणात्	१०६	བལྟོས་པའི་ཕྱིར་རོ
अपेक्षित	१०८	བལྟོས་པའི

अपेक्षित परव्यापार	१०८	གཞན་གྱི་བྱེད་པ་ལ་བལྟོས་པའི
अपोढ़	१०३	བྲལ་ཞིང
अप्रतिबद्ध ...	१०५, १०६ ...	ཐོགས་པ་མེད་པ
अप्रतिबद्ध ...	१०५	འབྲེལ་བ་མེད་པའི
अप्रतिबद्धस्य ...	१०५	མ་འབྲེལ་ན
अप्रदर्शित ...	११६, ११८ ...	རབ་ཏུ་མ་བསྟན་པ་ནི
अप्रदर्शित व्यतिरेक	११८	ལྡོག་པ་རབ་ཏུ་མ་བསྟན་པ་ནི
अप्रदर्शितान्वय ...	११६	རྗེས་སུ་འགྲོ་བ་རབ་ཏུ་མ་བསྟན་པ་ནི
अभाव	१०४, १०६, १०७, ११३, ११४	མེད་པ
अभाव	१०५	དངོས་པོ་མེད་པ
अभावत्वात् ...	११७	མེད་པ་ཉིད་ཀྱི་ཕྱིར་རོ
अभाववत्	११२	མེད་པ་ལྟ་བུའོ
अभावस्य	१०९	མེད་པར
अभावात्	१०५, १०६, १०८, ११२	མེད་པའི་ཕྱིར
अभावात्	१०५, १०९, ११३, ११४	མེད་པའི་ཕྱིར་རོ
अभावे	१०९, ११६ ...	མེད་ན
अभिधानात् ...	११०	བརྗོད་པའི་ཕྱིར
अभिमत	१११	འདོད་པ

अर्थापत्त्या ...	... ११८ ...	... དོན་གྱི་དབང་གིས
अर्थे ...	... १०५ ...	... དོན་ལ
अर्थेषु ...	... ११५ ...	... དོན་རྣམས་ལ
अवगन्तव्याः	... १०८ ...	... ཁོང་དུ་ཆུད་པར་བྱ་སྟེ
अवद्य ...	... १११ ...	... ཁ་ན་མ་ཐོ་བ་མེད་པར
अवयव ...	... ११६ ...	... ཡན་ལག་ནི
अवश्य ...	... ११० ...	... ངེས་པ
अवस्थित ...	... ११५ ...	... གནས་པ
अविकल ...	... ११३ ...	... མ་ཚང་བ་མེད་པར
अविद्यमान	... ११५ ...	... མེད་དོ
अविद्यमान	... ११७ ...	... བྲལ་བའི
अविरुद्ध ...	... ११३ ...	... མི་འགལ་བ
अवीत ...	... ११७ ...	... བྲལ་བ་མ
अवीतरागत्व	... ११७ ...	... འདོད་ཆགས་དང་མ་བྲལ་བ་ཉིད
अव्यतिरेक	... ११८ ...	... ལྡོག་པ་མེད་པ
अव्यतिरेक	... ११७ ...	... ལྡོག་པ་མེད་པ་ནི
अव्यतिरेक्रियाः	... ११७ ...	... མི་ལྡོག་པ་ཅན་དག
अव्यभिचार	... १०५ ...	... མི་འཁྲུལ་པར
अव्यभिचारी	... ११५ ...	... མི་འཁྲུལ་པ་ཅན
अश्रावण्या ...	... १११ ...	... མཉན་དུ་མི་རུང་ངོ་
असंस्कृत ...	... ११३ ...	... འདུས་པ་མ་ཡིན་པ

असत्	...	... १०९, ११६	...	མེད་པ
असत्	...	... १०८, ११०	...	མེད་པའི
असत्	...	... ११० ...	...	མེད་དོ
असति	...	... १०९, ११६	...	མེད་ན
असति	...	... १०९ ...	...	མེད་ན་ནི
असत्त्व	...	... ११४ ...	...	མེད
असत्त्व	...	... १०४, ११३	...	མེད་པ
असत्त्व	...	... ११८ ...	...	མེད་པ་ཉིད
असत्त्व	...	... ११३ ...	...	མེད་པའོ
असत्त्वस्य	...	... ११२ ...	...	མེད་པའི
असन्निधान		... १०३ ...	...	མི་ཉེ་བ་དག
असपक्ष	...	... १०४, १०९, ११६		མི་མཐུན་པའི་ཕྱོགས
असपक्ष	...	... १०४ ...	...	མི་མཐུན་པའི་ཕྱོགས་ནི
असपक्षे	...	... ११२, ११३	...	མི་མཐུན་པའི་ཕྱོགས་ལ
असम्भव	...	... ११६ ...	...	མི་སྲིད་དེ
असम्भवात्		... ११३ ...	...	མི་སྲིད་པའི་ཕྱིར
असम्भवात्		... १०५, ११५	...	མི་སྲིད་པའི་ཕྱིར་རོ
असर्वज्ञ	...	... ११३, ११६	...	ཐམས་ཅད་མཁྱེན་པ་མ
असिद्ध	...	... १११ ...	...	མ་གྲུབ
असिद्ध	...	... ११२, ११५	...	མ་གྲུབ་པ
असिद्ध	...	... ११२ ...	...	མ་གྲུབ་པའི
असिद्ध	...	... ११२ ...	...	མ་གྲུབ་པའོ

असिद्ध ...	... ११४	མ་གྲུབ་པ
असिद्ध ...	... ११२	མ་གྲུབ་པ་ཡིན་ཏེ
असिद्ध ...	... ११२	མ་གྲུབ་སྟེ
असिद्धत्वात्	... ११०	མ་གྲུབ་པའི་ཕྱིར
असिद्धि ...	... १११, ११२, ११४	མ་གྲུབ་པ
असिद्धेः ...	... ११४, ११८ ...	མ་གྲུབ་པའི་ཕྱིར
असिद्धेः ...	... १०७, १०९, ११३	མི་འགྲུབ་པའི་ཕྱིར་རོ
असिद्धौ ...	... ११२	མ་གྲུབ་ན
अस्ति ...	... १०९	ཡོད་དོ
अस्य ...	... १०३	དེའི
अस्य ...	... १०६	འདི་ན
अस्य ...	... ११६	དེའི

आ ।

आकाश ...	... ११५, ११६, ११७, ११८	ནམ་མཁའ
आक्षिप्त ...	... १०९	བསྐུས་པ
आख्यान ...	... १०८, १११ ...	བརྗོད་པ་སྟེ
आगम ...	... ११५	ལུང
आग्रह ...	... ११७	ཀུན་ཏུ་འཛིན་པ
आत्मन् ...	... १०३, १०५ ...	རང
आत्मन् ...	... १११, ११२, ११३, ११४, ११५	བདག

Sanskrit	Page	Tibetan
आसन	१११, ११३	སྟན
आह	११०	སྨྲས་ན
आह	११०	སྨྲས་པ
आहित	१०३	བསྐྱེད་པའི

इ।

Sanskrit	Page	Tibetan
इच्छता	१११	འདོད་པས
इतर	११६	གཞན་པ
इतर	१११	ཅིག་ཤོས་ནི
इतरयोः	११४	ཅིག་ཤོས་ལ
इति	११७	ལྟ་བུ་སྟེ
इति	१०८	ལྟ་བུའོ་ཞེས་བྱ་བ་ནི
इति	११०, १११	དེ་ལྟར་ན
इति	१०९, ११०, १११	ཞེས
इति	१०४	ཞེས་པ་ལྟ་བུ
इति	१०५	ཞེས་པ་ལྟ་བུའོ
इति	१०९	ཞེས་བྱ་སྟེ
इति	१११, ११३, ११६	ཞེས་བྱ་བ
इति	१०४	ཞེས་བྱ་བ་ལྟ་བུ
इति	१०८, १०९, ११०, १११, ११६	ཞེས་བྱ་བ་ནི
इति	११५	ཞེས་བྱ་བ་ལྟ་བུ་ཡིན་ལ

उ ।

उक्त	१०५	སྐད་སྨྲོས་པ
उक्त	११६	སྐད་སྨྲོས་པའི
उक्त	१११	བསྟན་པར
उक्त	११५	སྨྲོས་ཏེ
उक्त	११५, ११८	སྨྲོས་པ
उक्त	१०९	སྨྲོས་པ་ཡིན་ནོ
उक्त	११४	སྨྲས་པ
उक्त	११३	སྨྲས་ཞེ་ན
उक्त	११५	བཤད་དོ
उक्त	११५	བཤད་ན
उक्त	१०७	བཤད་པ
उक्तं	११६	བཤད་པ་ལ
उक्तमात्र	१११	སྨྲས་པ་ཙམ
उक्ति	११८	སྨྲས་པ་ནི
उक्ते	११०	བསྟན་པར
उक्ते	११०	བསྟན་པས
उक्तौ	१११	སྨྲས
उक्तौ	११६	བཤད་དེ
उच्यते	११६	བརྗོད་དེ
उत्पत्तिमत्	११२	སྐྱེ་བ་ཅན
उत्पत्तिमत्	१०८, १०९	སྐྱེ་བ་དང་ལྡན་པ

उत्पत्तेः ...	... ༡༠༥ ...	... བྱུང་བའི་ཕྱིར
उदाहरण ...	... ༡༡༤,༡༡༧	... དཔེ་ནི
उद्भावन ...	... ༡༡༨ ...	... བརྗོད་པ་ནི
उद्भावनानि	... ༡༡༨ ...	... བརྗོད་པ་དག་ནི
उपचारात्	... ༡༠༨ ...	... བཏགས་པའི་ཕྱིར་རོ
उपदर्शन ...	... ༡༠༩ ...	... བསྟན་པ
उपदर्शन ...	... ༡༠༨ ...	... ཉེ་བར་སྟོན་པའོ
उपदिश्यमान	... ༡༡༢ ...	... བསྙབས་པ
उपदिष्टवान्	... ༡༡༧ ...	... བསྟན་ཏེ
उपन्यस्त ...	... ༡༡༡ ...	... བཀོད་པ
उपयान्ति ...	... ༡༠༦ ...	... འགྱུར་རོ
उपल ...	... ༡༡༧ ...	... རྡོ
उपलखण्ड ...	... ༡༡༧ ...	... རྡོའི་དུམ་བུ
उपलब्धि ...	... ༡༠༤, ༡༠༥, ༡༠༦, ༡༠༧, ༡༠༨, ༡༠༩, ༡༡༠, ༡༡༥	དམིགས་པ
उपलब्धि ...	... ༡༠༥, ༡༠༦	དམིགས་པ་ནི
उपलब्धि ...	... ༡༠༩ ...	... དམིགས་སོ
उपलभमान	... ༡༡༢ ...	... དམིགས་པའི
उपलभ्यते ...	... ༡༠༨, ༡༡༠, ༡༡༥	དམིགས་པ
उपलभ्यते ...	... ༡༡༠ ...	... དམིགས་པ་འགྱུར་ན
उपलभ्यते ...	... ༡༠༩ ...	... དམིགས་པར་འགྱུར་ཏེ
उपलभ्यते ...	... ༡༠༨, ༡༡༠, ༡༡༥	དམིགས་སོ

उपलभ्यते	... ...	११२	ཡིན་ནོ
उपलम्भ	... ...	१०४	དམིགས་པ
उपलम्भ	... ...	१०४	རྙེད
उपसंहार	...	११५	སྟོན་པ
उपाधि	... ...	१०८	ཁྱད་པར
उभय	... ...	११७	གཉི་ག
उभय	... ...	११६	གཉིས་ཀ
उभयव्यतिरेक	...	११७	གཉི་ག་ལས་ལྡོག་པ
उभयासिद्ध	...	११२	གཉི་ག་ལ་མ་གྲུབ་པ
उष्मा	... ...	११३	ཚ་བའི

ऋ।

ऋषभ	... ...	११७	ཁྱུ་མཆོག

ए।

एक	... ...	१०६, १११, ११२, ११४	གཅིག
एक	... ...	१०४, ११४ ...	གཅིག་ནི
एकत्र	... ...	११४, ११५ ...	གཅིག་ལ
एकदेशे	... ...	११२	ཕྱོགས་གཅིག་ལ
एकात्मनि	... ...	११४	བདག་གཅིག་ལ
एकादश	... ...	१०५	བཅུ་གཅིག
एकैकस्य	... ...	११४ ...	རེ་རེ (gen.)
एतत्	... ...	१११	དེ

क।

कथयता	१०९	བརྗོད་པས
कपिल	११७	སེར་སྐྱ
कयोः	११३	གང་ཞེ་ན
कर्म	११६, ११७	ལས
कल्पना	१०३	རྟོག་པ
कल्पना	१०३	རྟོག་པ་ནི
कल्पनापोढ़	१०३	རྟོག་པ་དང་བྲལ་ཞིང་
कश्चित्	१०८, ११७	འགའ་ཞིག
कश्चित्	१०८, ११४, ११६	ཅི་ཡང་
कश्चित्	११२	ལ་ལ་ཞིག
कस्मात्	११३	ཅིའི་ཕྱིར
कारण	१०५, १०६, १०७, १०९, ११३	རྒྱུ
कारणे	१०८	རྒྱུ་ལ
कारेण	११०	བྱེད་པས
कार्य्यं	१०४, १०५, १०६, १०७, १०८, १०९, ११३, ११५, ११६	འབྲས་བུ
कार्य्यं	१०४, १०९	འབྲས་བུ་ནི
कार्य्यता	११६	འབྲས་བུ་ཉིད
कार्य्यहेतु	१०९	འབྲས་བུའི་གཏན་ཚིགས
काल	१०५	དུས

ख ।

ग ।

ग्राह्यवचन	११७	ཚིག་གཟུང་བར་བྱ
ग्राह्यवचन	११७	ཚིག་གཟུང་བར་བྱ་བ

घ ।

घट	१०४, १०८, १०९, ११०, ११५, ११६	བུམ་པ

च ।

च	१०५	ཀྱང་
च	१०३, १०४, १०५, १०७, १०८, १०९, ११६	དང་
च	११८	དམ
च	१०५, १०६, १०७, १०९, ११०, ११३, ११४, ११५, ११६	ཡང་
च	१०४	ཡང་ནི
च	११४	འམ
चक्षुः	१११, ११२	མིག
चतुर्	१०३	བཞིས་སྡེ
चतुर्विध	१०३	རྣམ་པ་བཞི་སྡེ
चत्वारः	१११	བཞི
चाक्षुषत्व	११०, ११२	མིག་གིས་གཟུང་བ་ཉིད་ནི
चित्त	१०३	སེམས
चेतनाः	११२	སེམས་ཡོད་པར (nom.)
चैत्त	१०३	སེམས་ལས་བྱུང་བ

ज।

जनयतः	११५	སྐྱེད་པར་བྱེད་དོ
जनित	१०३	བསྐྱེད་པའི
जन्म	११६	སྐྱེ་བ
जातयः	११८	ལྟག་གཅོད་རྣམས
जात्युत्तराणि	११८	ལྟག་གཅོད་རྣམས
जिज्ञासित	१०४	ཤེས་པར་འདོད་པའི
जीवत्	११४	གསོན་པོའི
ज्ञान	१०३, १०४, ११७	ཤེས་པ
ज्ञान	१०२	ཤེས་པ་ནི
ज्योतिः	११७	སྐར་མ

त।

तत्	१०३, १०५, १०८, १०९, ११०, १११, ११२, ११६	དེ
तत्	१०५, ११५	དེ་དང་
तत्	१०३, १०८, १०९, ११०, १११, ११३, ११५, ११६, ११८	དེ་ནི
तत्	१०३, १०८, ११२; ११५, ११६	དེའི
तद्	११८	དེའི་ཕྱིར
तद्	१०५	དེར
ततः	१०४	དེ་ལས

तत्र	१०५	དེ་དང་
तत्र	१०९, ११५, ११६	དེ་ན
तत्र	१०३, १०४, १०८, १११, ११४	དེ་ལ
तत्र	११५	འདིར
तथा	११०	དེ་ནི
तथा	१०८, १०९, ११०, ११२, ११६, ११७	དེ་བཞིན་དུ
तथा	१०८	བཞིན་དེ
तद्भाव	१०४	དེ་མེད་པ
तदा	११०, १११	དེའི་ཚེ
तदुत्पत्ति	१०५, ११७	དེ་ལས་བྱུང་བ
तदेव	१०३	དེ་ཉིད
तद्यथा	११५, ११७	དཔེར་ན
तद्विरुद्ध	१०४	དེ་དང་འགལ་བ
तन्मात्र	११६	དེ་ཙམ་གྱི
तया	१०३	དེ་དང་
तयोः	१०८	དེ་དག (gen.)
तरवः	११२	ཤིང་རྣམས
तस्मात्	१०९, ११५	དེ་ལྟ་བས་ན
तस्मात्	११४	དེ་བས་ན
तस्मिन्	११०	དེ་ལ
तस्य	१०३, ११४, ११६	དེའི

तस्य ...	... ११७	དེ་ལ་ནི
तस्या एव ...	... १०५	དེ་ཉིད་ཀྱིས
तादात्म्य ...	... १०५, १०९ ...	དེའི་བདག་ཉིད
तादात्म्यात्	... १०८	དེའི་བདག་ཉིད་ཡིན་པའི་ཕྱིར་རོ
तादात्म्यात्	... १०५	རང་བཞིན་ཡིན་པའི་ཕྱིར་དེ
तादृश ...	... ११०	དེ་ལྟ་བུ
तादृश ...	... ११०	དེ་དྲ་བའི
तावतैव ...	... ११५	དེ་ཙམ་གྱིས
ताभ्यां ...	... ११४	དེ་གཉིས་དང
ताभ्यामेव ...	... १०५	དེ་གཉིས་ཁོ་ནས
तिमिर ...	... १०३	རབ་རིབ
तुषार ...	... १०६	བ་མོ
तृतीय ...	... ११३	གསུམ་པ
तृतीय ...	... १०८	གསུམ་པ་ནི
ते ...	... १०५	དེ་གཉིས
ते ...	... ११८	དེ་དག
ते ...	... १०७	དེ་དག་ནི
ते ...	... ११७	དེ་ནི
तेन ...	... १०९, ११०, ११८	དེས
तेन ...	... ११६	དེས་ན
त्रयाणां ...	... ११४	གསུམ་པོ་དག་ལས

Sanskrit			Page			Tibetan
त्रयाणां	...	...	१११	...	...	གསུམ་ལས
त्रयीविद्	...	...	११७	...	...	གསུམ་རིག་པ
त्रि	...	...	११५	...	...	གསུམ
त्रि	...	...	१०४, १०८		...	གསུམ་པ
त्रि	...	...	१०४	...	...	གསུམ་པོ
त्रिरूप	...	...	१०४, १०८		...	ཚུལ་གསུམ་པ
त्रिरूप	...	...	१०४	...	...	ཚུལ་གསུམ་པོ
त्रिरूप	...	...	१११	...	...	ཚུལ་གསུམ་པའི
त्रैरूप्य	...	...	१०४	...	...	ཚུལ་གསུམ་པ་ཉིད
त्वक्	...	...	११२	...	...	ཤུན་པ
त्वात्	...	...	१०६	...	...	ཉིད་ཀྱི་ཕྱིར་རོ
त्वात्	...	...	११४	...	...	ཕྱིར
त्वात्	...	...	१०३, १०४		...	ཡིན་པའི་ཕྱིར
त्वात्	...	...	१०५	...	...	ཡིན་པའི་ཕྱིར་རོ
त्वेन	...	...	११३	...	...	ཉིད་ཀྱིས

द ।

Sanskrit			Page			Tibetan
दग्ध	...	...	१०६	...	...	བཙུ་པོ
दर्शन	...	...	१०६	...	...	མཐོང་བ
दर्शनीय	...	...	१०९	...	...	བསྟན་པར་བྱའོ
दर्शनीय	...	...	११६	...	...	བཤད་པར་བྱའོ
दर्शनीयौ	...	...	११६	...	...	བསྟན་པར་བྱ་བར
दर्शयता	...	...	११६	...	...	སྟོན་པར་བྱེད་པས

दर्शयितुम्	११६, ११८	བསྟན་པར
दर्शित	११६	བསྟན་པ
दर्शित	१११	བསྟན་པར
दर्शिते	११६	བསྟན་པ་ན
दहन	१०६	གདུང་བར་བྱེད་པ
दूषणः	११८	སུན་འབྱིན་པ
दूषणाः	११८	སུན་འབྱིན་པ་དག
दूषणाभासाः	११८	སུན་འབྱིན་པ་ལྟར་སྣང་བ་དག་ནི
दृष्ट	१०८	མཐོང་བ
दृष्टान्त	११५, ११६	དཔེ
दृष्टान्ताभास	११८	དཔེ་ལྟར་སྣང་བ
देश	१०५, ११२, ११५	ཡུལ
दोष	११५, ११८	སྐྱོན
दोषाः	११६	ཉེས་པ་རྣམས
द्रष्टव्याः	१०८	ལྟ་བར་བྱའོ
द्वय	११०	གཉིས་ཀྱིས
द्वयोः	११०	གཉི་ག་ལ
द्वयोः	११४	གཉིས་ལས
द्वयोः	११४	དེ་གཉིས་ལ
द्वयोर्द्वयोः	११४	གཉིས་གཉིས་ལ
द्वि	११३	གཉིས

द्वि	... ... १०९	གཉིས་དེ
द्वि	... ... १०३	གཉིས་སྡེ
द्वि	... ... ११३	གཉིས་པ
द्वितीय	... ... ११५	གཉིས་པ
द्वितीय	... ... १०४	གཉིས་པ་ནི
द्वितीय	... ... १०७	གཉིས་པའོ
द्विविध	... ... १०३, १०८, ११३	རྣམ་པ་གཉིས་དེ
द्विविध	... ... ११३	རྣམ་པ་དེ་གཉི་ག
द्विधा	... ... १०४	རྣམ་པ་གཉིས་དེ
द्विप्रकार	... ... १०९	རྣམ་པ་གཉིས་དེ
द्वौ	... ... १०४	གཉིས་ནི

ध ।

धर्म	... ... १०४, १०८, ११०, ११२, ११६, ११७	ཆོས
धर्म	... ... ११२	ཆོས་ནི
धर्मशास्त्र	... ... ११७	ཆོས་ཀྱི་བསྟན་བཅོས
धर्मिन्	... ... १०४, ११०, ११२	ཆོས་ཅན
धर्मे	... ... ११२	ཆོས་སུ
धूम	... ... १०५, १०६, १०९, ११६	དུ་བ
धूम	... ... १०९	དུ་བ་ཡོད
धूमात्	... ... १०४, १०६ ...	དུ་བ་ཡོད་པའི་ཕྱིར
ध्रुव	... ... १०६	ངེས་པར

न।

न	१०८, ११२, ११३, ११४, ११५, ११६	མ
न	१०४, ११०, ११३	མ་ཡིན་ནེ
न	१०६, १११, ११३, ११५	མ་ཡིན་ནོ
न	११३	མ་ཡིན་པ
न	१०९, ११०, ११३, ११५, ११६, ११७, ११८	མི
न	१०४, १०५, १०६, ११४, ११६, ११७	མེད་དེ
न	१०५, १०६, १०८, ११०, ११४, ११५	མེད་དོ
न हि	१०९	མ་ཡིན་ནོ
नान्तरीयकत्वात्	११४	གདོན་མི་ཟ་བའི་ཕྱིར་རོ
नाम	११५	ཞེས་བྱ་བ
नास्ति	११५	མེད་དེ
नास्ति	११७	མེད་ན
नास्ति	११५	མེད་པ
नास्ति	१०९	མེད་པ་ཉིད་ཡིན་ན
निकुञ्ज	११२	རི་སུལ
नित्य	११६, ११८	རྟག་པ
नित्य	१११	རྟག་པའོ
नित्यत्व	११२, ११३	རྟག་པ་ཉིད

नियम ...	... १०५, ११६ ...	ངེས་པ
नियमेन ...	... १०९ ...	... ངེས་པར
निरस्त ...	... ११६ ...	... བསལ་བ
निराकृत ...	... १११ ...	... བསལ་བ་ནི
निराकृतस्य	... १११ ...	... བསལ་བ་ལས
निराकृताः ...	... १११ ...	... བསལ་བ
निराक्रियते	... १११ ...	... བསལ་བ་གང་ཡིན་པ
निरात्मक ...	... ११४ ...	... བདག་མེད་པ
निरात्मकत्वेन	... ११४ ...	... བདག་མེད་པར
निरात्मकात्	... ११४ ...	... བདག་མེད་པ་ལས
निरास ...	... ११८ ...	... བསལ་བར
निरोध ...	... ११२ ...	... འགགས་པ
निर्देश्य ...	... १०६ ...	... བསྟན་ཏོ
निर्देश्य ...	... ११० ...	... བསྟན་པར
निर्देश्य ...	... ११० ...	... བསྟན་པར་བྱ་ཞེ་ན
निवृत्ति ...	... १०५, १०७	... ལོག
निवृत्ति ...	... १०५ ...	... ལོག་ན
निवृत्ति ...	... १०७ ...	... ལོག་པ
निवृत्ति ...	... १०६ ...	... ལྡོག་པ
निवृत्तौ ...	... १०६, ११३	... ལོག་པས
निश्चय ...	... १०५, ११४	... ངེས་པ
निश्चयस्य ...	... ११४ ...	... ངེས་ན

निश्चयात् ... ... १०५ ... ... ངེས་པའི་ཕྱིར་རོ

निश्चयेन ... ... ११८ ... ... ངེས་པར

निश्चित ... ... १०४ ... ... ངེས་པའོ

निष्पत्तौ ... ... १०८ ... ... གྲུབ་པ་ལ

निष्पत्तौ ... ... १०८ ... ... འགྲུབ་པར་བྱེད་པའི་ཕྱིར

नील ... ... १०९ ... ... སྔོན་པོ

नौ ... ... १०३ ... ... གྲུ

नौयान ... ... १०३ ... ... གྲུར་ཞུགས་པ

न्यायबिन्दु ... ... १०३, ११८ ... རིགས་པའི་ཐིགས་པ

न्यूनता ... ... ११८ ... ... མ་ཚང་བ

न्यूनता ... ... ११८ ... ... མ་ཚང་བ་ཉིད

प।

पक्ष ... ... १०८, ११०, १११ ཕྱོགས

पक्ष ... ... १११ ... ... ཕྱོགས་ཡིན་དེ

पक्ष ... ... ११० ... ... ཕྱོགས་སོ

पक्षाभासाः ... १११ ... ... ཕྱོགས་ལྟར་སྣང་བ

पदार्थानां ... ... ११२ ... ... དངོས་པོ་རྣམས་ཀྱི

पर ... ... ११८ ... ... ཕ་རོལ་པོ

पर ... ... १०८ ... ... གཞན་གྱི

परमाणु ... ... ११६, ११७ ... རྡུལ་ཕྲ་རབ

परमार्थ ... ... १०३ ... ... དོན་དམ་པ

परमार्थसत् ... १०३ ... ... དོན་དམ་པར་ཡོད་པ

परस्पर ...	... ११३ ...	...	གཅིག་གིས་གཅིག
परस्पर ...	... ११५ ...	...	ཕན་ཚུན
परार्थ ...	... १०४ ...	...	གཞན་གྱི་དོན
परार्थ ...	... १११, ११२	...	གཞན་གྱི་དོན་བྱེད་དེ
परार्थानुमान	... १०८, १११	...	གཞན་གྱི་དོན་གྱི་རྗེས་སུ་དཔག་པ་ནི
परिग्रह ...	... ११७ ...	...	ཡོངས་སུ་འཛིན་པ
परिच्छेद ...	... १०३, १०४, १०८		ལེའུ
परिच्छेद ...	... १०३, १०७	...	ལེའུ་སྟེ
परिहार ...	... ११३ ...	...	སྤངས་ཏེ
पर्यन्त ...	... १०३ ...	...	མཐའ
पर्यन्तज ...	... १०३ ...	...	མཐའ་ལས་བྱུང་བའི
पारम्पर्येण	... १०६ ...	...	བརྒྱུད་པའི་སྒོ་ནས
पारार्थ्य ...	... ११२ ...	...	གཞན་གྱི་དོན་བྱེད་པར
पुनः ...	... ११६ ...	...	ཡང
पुरुष ...	... १०३ ...	...	སྐྱེས་བུ
पुरुष ...	... ११२, ११६, ११७		མི
पुरुषवान् ...	... १०६ ...	...	མི་དང་ལྡན་པ
पूर्वं ...	... ११८ ...	...	སྔར
पूर्विका ...	... १०३ ...	...	སྔོན་དུ་འགྲོ་བ་ཅན
पृथक् ...	... ११५, ११६	...	ལོགས་ཤིག་ཏུ
प्रकर्ष ...	... १०३ ...	...	རབ

प्रत्ययान्तर	१०४	རྐྱེན་གཞན
प्रथम	१०३	དང་པོ
प्रथम	१०३	དང་པོ་ནི
प्रदेश	१०४, १०८	ཕྱོགས
प्रदर्शनार्थम्	१११	བསྟན་པའི་ཕྱིར་དེ
प्रमाण	१०३, १०४, १०७, १०८, १११, ११७	ཚད་མ
प्रमेयत्व	११२	གཞལ་བྱ་ཉིད
प्रयत्न	११३	བརྩལ
प्रयुक्तेन	१०६	བརྗོད་པས
प्रयोग	१०५, १०६, १०८, ११०, ११५	སྦྱོར་བ
प्रयोग	१०६	སྦྱོར་བ་ནི
प्रयोग	१०८, १०६	སྦྱོར་བའོ
प्रयोगे	१०६, ११०	སྦྱོར་བ་ལ
प्रवृत्त	११५	ཞུགས་པ་ཡིན་པས་ན
प्रसिद्धे	११४	སྒྲུབ་པ་ལ
प्राण	११४	སྲོག
प्राणादिमत्त्वात्	११४	སྲོག་ལ་སོགས་པ་དང་ལྡན་པའི་ཕྱིར

फ ।

फल	१०३, १०४	འབྲས་བུ

ब ।

बल	११५	སྟོབས
बाष्प	११२	རླངས་པ
ब्राह्मण	११७	བྲམ་ཟེ་ནི

भ ।

भवतः	११३	འབྱུང་བ་ལ
भवति	१०९	འགྱུར་པས
भवति	१०४	འགྱུར་བའོ
भवति	११०, १११	འགྱུར་རོ
भवति	१०९	འབྱུང་བ
भवति	११६	ཡིན་ཏེ
भवति	१०९	ཡིན་ལ
भवति	१११, ११३, ११८	ཡིན་ནོ
भवन्ति	११६	ཡིན་ཏེ
भवन्ति	१११	ཡིན་ནོ
भाव	१०८	ངོ་བོ
भाव	१०८	ངོ་བོ་ནི
भाव	१०६, ११३	དངོས་པོ
भाव	१०७, ११२	ཡོད་པ
भाव	११४	ཡོད་པར
भावना	१०३	བསྒོམས་པ
भाविन्	१०४	གྱུར་པ

Sanskrit	Page	Tibetan
भावी	१०६	འགྱུར
भावे	१०९	དངོས་པོར
भावेन	११२	དངོས་པོར
भिद्यते (भिन्न)	११४	ཐ་དད་པ
भूत	१०८	གྱུར་པའི
भूत	११२	འབྱུང་བ
भूत	१०६	འབྱུང་བའི
भूत	१०३	ཡང་དག་པའི
भूतार्थ	१०३	ཡང་དག་པའི་དོན
भेद	१०६	ཐ་དད
भेद	१०८	བྱེ་བྲག
भेदात्	१०५, १०८	བྱེ་བྲག་གིས
भेदित्व	१०८	ཐ་དད་པ་ཅན་ཉིད
भेदेन	१०८	བྱེ་བྲག་གིས
भेदेन	१०८	བྱེ་བྲག་གིས་ཏེ
भ्यां	१०६	དག་གིས
भ्रमण	१०३	བསྐོར་བ
भ्रान्त्या	११५	འཁྲུལ་པས

म ।

Sanskrit	Page	Tibetan
मत्त्वात्	११६	ལྡན་པའི་ཕྱིར
मत्त्वात्	११७	ལྡན་པའི་ཕྱིར་རོ
मनः	१०३	ཡིད

Sanskrit	Page	Tibetan
यत्	११५	གང་ཞིག
यत्	१०९	གང་ཡིན་པ
यत्र	१०९, ११५, ११६	གང་ན
यत्र	१११, ११४, ११७	གང་ལ
यथा	१०४, १०५, १०६, १०८, १०९, ११०, १११, ११२, ११३, ११४, ११५, ११६, ११७	དཔེར་ན
यथा	१०८	ཇི་ལྟ་བུ་དག་གིས
यथायोगं	११४	ཇི་རིགས་པར
यथावस्थित	११५	ཇི་ལྟ་བ་དེ་བཞིན་དུ་གནས་པར
यथास्वं प्रमाणैः	१०८	རང་གི་ཚད་མ་ཇི་ལྟ་བུ་དག་གིས
यथोक्त	१०५	ཇི་སྐད་སྨོས་པ
यथोक्त	११६	ཇི་སྐད་སྨོས་པའི
यदि	११०	གལ་ཏེ
यद्यपि	११७	གལ་ཏེ
यस्मात्	११०	འདིར
यान	१०३	ཀྱུགས་པ
युक्त	१०६	དང་ལྡན་པའི
युगपत्	११५	ཅིག་ཅར་དུ

र।

ल ।

लक्षण	१०३, १११, ११२, ११५, ११६, ११८	མཚན་ཉིད
लक्षणा	१०३	མཚན་ཉིད་དེ
लक्षणा	१०३, १०७	མཚན་ཉིད་ནི
लक्षणता	११३	མཚན་ཉིད་ཁོ་ན་སྟེ
लक्षणप्राप्त	१०४, १०७, १०८, १०९, ११०, ११५	རིག་བྱར་གྱུར་པ
लक्षणप्राप्तस्य	१०५	རིག་བྱར་གྱུར་པ་ལས
लक्षणप्राप्ति	१०४	རིག་བྱར་གྱུར་པ་ནི
लिङ्ग	१०४, १०५, १०८, १०९, १११	རྟགས
लिङ्ग	१०४, ११६	རྟགས་ནི
लिङ्गभूत	११७	རྟགས་སུ་གྱུར་པ

व ।

वक्तव्य	१०९	བརྗོད་པར་བྱའོ
वक्तृ	११२, ११३, ११६, ११७	སྨྲ་བ
वक्तृत्व	११३	སྨྲ་བ་ཉིད
वक्तृत्वात्	११४, ११७	སྨྲ་བའི་ཕྱིར
वक्तृत्वात्	११६	སྨྲ་བའི་ཕྱིར་ན
वचन	१११, ११३, ११४	ཚིག
वचन	१०९	ཚིག་གིས་ནི
वचनेन	१११	ཚིག་ཏུ

विचारेषु ... ... ११५ ... ... དཔྱད་པ་དག་ལ

विज्ञान ... ... १०३, ११२ ... རྣམ་པར་ཤེས་པ

विधा ... ... १०३ ... ... རྣམ་པ

विधि ... ... १०६ ... ... ཡོད་པ

विधेः ... ... ११३ ... ... ཡོད་པའི་ཕྱིར

विनाश ... ... १०६ ... ... འཇིག་པ་ནི

विपक्ष ... ... ११२, ११८ ... མི་མཐུན་པའི་ཕྱོགས

विपक्षयोः ... ... ११६ ... ... མི་མཐུན་པའི་ཕྱོགས་དག་ལ

विपरीत ... ... ११६ ... ... ཕྱིན་ཅི་ལོག་ནི

विपरीत व्यतिरेक ... ११८ ... ... ལྡོག་པ་ཕྱིན་ཅི་ལོག་ནི

विपरीतस्य ... ११५ ... ... ལོག་པར

विपरीतान्वय ... ११६ ... ... རྗེས་སུ་འགྲོ་བ་ཕྱིན་ཅི་
ལོག་ནི

विपर्यय ... ... ११३ ... ... ཕྱིན་ཅི་ལོག

विपर्यय ... ... १११ ... ... བཟློག་པ་ནི

विपर्यय ... ... ११४ ... ... ལོག་པར

विपर्ययात् ... ... ११३ ... ... ལྡོག་པ་ལས

विप्रकर्षात् ... ११४ ... ... བསྐལ་བ་ཡིན་པའི་ཕྱིར

विप्रकृष्ट ... ... १०५, १०७ ... བསྐལ་པའི

विभ्रम ... ... १०३ ... ... འཁྲུལ་པ

विभ्रम ... ... ११२ ... ... མི་རྟོགས་པ

विषय ... ... १०३, १०७, १०८, ११०, ११३ ཡུལ

विषय ... ... १०३ ... ... ཡུལ་ནི

विषय ... ... ११० ... ... ཡུལ་ཡིན

विषये ... ... ११५ ... ... ཡུལ་ལ

विषाण ... ... १०८ ... ... རྭ

वीत ... ... ११७ ... ... བྲལ་བ

वीतत्व ... ... ११७ ... ... བྲལ་བ་ཉིད

वीतराग ... ... ११४, ११७ ... འདོད་ཆགས་དང་བྲལ་བ

वीतरागयोः ... ११४ ... ... འདོད་ཆགས་དང་བྲལ་བ་དག་ནི

वृक्ष ... ... १०५ ... ... ཤིང་

वृक्ष ... ... १०४ ... ... ཤིང་ངོ་

वृत्ति ... ... ११४ ... ... གནས་པ

वृत्ति ... ... ११४ ... ... གནས་པར

वेदितव्य ... ... १०७, ११८ ... རིག་པར་བྱའོ

वैधर्म्य ... ... ११७, ११८ ... ཆོས་མི་མཐུན་པ

वैधर्म्य ... ... १०९, ११० ... ཆོས་མི་མཐུན་པ་ཉིད

वैधर्म्य ... ... ११७ ... ... ཆོས་མི་མཐུན་པའི

वैधर्म्यवत् ... ... १०८ ... ... ཆོས་མི་མཐུན་པ་ཉིད་ཅན་ནོ

वैधर्म्यवतः ... ... १०९ ... ... ཆོས་མི་མཐུན་པ་ཉིད་ཅན་གྱི

वैधर्म्येण ... ... १०९, ११७ ... ཆོས་མི་མཐུན་པས

व्यावृत्तत्वेन	११४	ལྡོག་པ་ཉིད་དུ
व्यावृत्तया	११८	ལྡོག་པ་ཡོད་མེད་ཀྱི
व्यावृत्ति	११३	ལྡོག་པ་ནི
व्यावृत्तिक	११२	ལྡོག་པ་ལ
व्युत्पाद्यते	१०३	བསྟན་ཏོ

श ।

शक्य	११८	ནུས་ཏེ
शक्य	११६	ནུས་སོ
शब्द	११०, १११, ११२	སྒྲ
शब्द	१०८, १०९, १११, ११६, ११८	སྒྲ་ནི
शब्दे	११०	སྒྲ་ལ
शयन	१११, ११३	མལ་ཆ
शरीर	११४	ལུས
शरीर	११४	ལུས་ནི
शश	१०८	རི་བོང
शशविषाण	१०८	རི་བོང་གི་རྭ
शशी	१११	རི་བོང་ཅན
शासन	११७	བསྟན་པ
शास्त्र	११०, ११७	བསྟན་བཅོས
शास्त्रकाराणां	११५	བསྟན་བཅོས་བྱེད་པ་རྣམས་ནི (gen.)

स ।

सः	१०७, १०८, ११०, १११, ११५, ११६, ११७	དེ་ནི
सत्	१०३, १०८, १०९, ११६	ཡོད་པ
सत्	११०	ཡོད་པའི
सत्	१०४, १०९, ११०	ཡོད་ལ
सति	१०५	ཡོད་ན
सत्ता	१०४	ཡོད་པ
सत्त्व	११४	ཡོད
सत्त्व	१०४, ११३, ११६, ११८	ཡོད་པ
सत्सु	१०४	ཡོད་ན
सन्दिग्ध	११३	ཐེ་ཚོམ་དུ་གྱུར་པ་ཡིན་ཏེ
सन्दिग्ध	११६, ११७ ...	ཐེ་ཚོམ་ཟ་བ
सन्दिग्ध	११७	ཐེ་ཚོམ་ཟ་བ་ནི
सन्दिग्ध	११३	ཐེ་ཚོམ་ཟ་བ་དང་ལྡན་པའི
सन्दिग्ध	११४	ཐེ་ཚོམ་ཟ་བ་ཡིན་ཏེ
सन्दिग्ध	११२	ཐེ་ཚོམ་ཟ་བ་ཡིན་ནོ
सन्दिग्ध	११४	ཐེ་ཚོམ་ཟ་བའི
सन्दिग्धसाधनव्यतिरेक	११७	སྒྲུབ་པ་ལས་ལྡོག་པ་ལ་ཐེ་ཚོམ་ཟ་བ་ནི
सन्दिग्धसाध्यव्यतिरेक	११७	བསྒྲུབ་པར་བྱ་བ་ལས་ལྡོག་པ་ལ་ཐེ་ཚོམ་ཟ་བ

सर्वगत	११५	ཐམས་ཅད་ན་གནས་པ
सर्वगत	११२	ཐམས་ཅད་ན་གནས་པར
सर्वज्ञ	११२, ११३, ११४, ११७	ཐམས་ཅད་མཁྱེན་པ
सर्वज्ञत्व	११३	ཐམས་ཅད་མཁྱེན་པ་ཉིད
सर्वतः	११६	ཐམས་ཅད་ལས
सर्वत्र	११२	ཐམས་ཅད་ན
सर्वत्र	११२, ११८	ཐམས་ཅད་ལ
सर्वत्र	१०६	དེ་དག་ཐམས་ཅད་ལ
सर्वस्मात्	११४	ཐམས་ཅད་ལས
सर्वस्य	१०९	ཐམས་ཅད་ཀྱི
सर्वे	१०६, १०८	ཐམས་ཅད་ནི
सहकारिन्	१०३	ལྷན་ཅིག་བྱེད་པ་ཅན
सा	१०५	དེ་ནི
सांख्य	११२	གྲངས་ཅན
साकल्य	१०४	ཚང་བ་ཉིད
सात्मक	११४	བདག་བཅས་པ
सात्मक	११४	བདག་དང་བཅས་པ
साधन	१०४, ११०, १११, ११७, ११८	སྒྲུབ་པ
साधन	१०८, ११५, ११७	སྒྲུབ་པའི
साधन	११४	སྒྲུབ་པས
साधन	११६, ११७	སྒྲུབ་པར་བྱེད་པ

साध्यधर्म ...	... १०४	བསྒྲུབ་པར་བྱ་བ
साधर्म्यवत् ...	... १०८, ११० ...	ཆོས་མཐུན་པ་ཉིད་ཅན
साधर्म्यवत् ...	... १०८	ཆོས་མཐུན་པ་ཉིད་ཅན་ནི
साध्ये ...	... ११२, ११३ ...	བསྒྲུབ་པ་ལ
साध्ये ...	... १०९, ११० ...	བསྒྲུབ་པར་བྱ་བ་ལ
सामर्थ्य ...	... १०३, १०५, १०६	ནུས་པ་ཁོ་ན
सामर्थ्यात् ...	... ११०	ཤུགས་ཀྱིས
सामर्थ्यात् ...	... ११०	ཤུགས་ཉིད་ཀྱིས
सामान्य ...	... ११५, ११८ ...	སྤྱི
सामान्य ...	... १०३	སྤྱིའི
सामान्यलक्षण	... ११८	སྤྱིའི་མཚན་ཉིད
सामान्येन ...	... १०४	སྤྱི་དང་
सारूप्य ...	... १०२	འདྲ་བ་ཉིད
सिद्ध ...	... १०८	གྲུབ་སྟེ
सिद्ध ...	... १०८, १०९, १११	གྲུབ་པ
सिद्धि ...	... १११, ११३ ...	གྲུབ་པ
सिद्धि ...	... ११३	གྲུབ་པ་ནི
सिद्धि ...	... ११०	གྲུབ་བོ
सिद्धि ...	... १०३, १०५, ११८	འགྲུབ་པ
सिद्धि ...	... १०५	འགྲུབ་བོ
सिद्धेः ...	... १०३	འགྲུབ་པའི་ཕྱིར
सिद्धौ ...	... ११२	བསྒྲུབ་པར་བྱ་བ་ལ

सुख	११२	བདེ་བ
स्थित	११०	བརྟེན་ཏེ
स्थित	११३	གནས་པའི
स्थितसाधन	११०	བརྟེན་ཏེ་སྒྲུབ་པ
स्थिति	११५	འདུག་པ
स्पर्श	१०५, १०६, ११३	རེག་པ
स्मृति	१०५	དྲན་པ
स्व	१०३, १०४	རང་
स्व	१०८, १११	རང་གི
स्व	११५	རང་དང་
स्वभाव	१०४, १०५, १०६, १०८, १०९, ११५, ११६	རང་བཞིན
स्वभाव	१०४	རང་བཞིན་ནི
स्वभावता	११५	རང་བཞིན་ཉིད
स्वभावत्व	१०८	རང་བཞིན་ཉིད
स्वभावत्वात्	१०८	རང་བཞིན་ཡིན་པའི་ཕྱིར
स्वभावभूत	१०८	རང་བཞིན་དུ་གྱུར་པའི
स्वभावयोः	११६	རང་བཞིན་གཉིས་ནི (gen.)
स्वभावस्य	१०८	རང་བཞིན་ཡང་
स्वभावहेतु	११५	རང་བཞིན་གྱི་གཏན་ཚིགས
स्वभावेन	११६	རང་བཞིན་གྱིས
स्वयम्	१०६, ११०, ११२	བདག་ཉིད

स्वयम्	१११	བདག་ཉིད་ཀྱིས
स्वयं	११२	བདག་ཉིད་ལ
स्वयमिष्ट	११०	བདག་ཉིད་དང་འདོད་པ
स्वरूप	११०	རང་གི་ངོ་བོ
स्वरूपेण	१११	ངོ་བོར
स्वलक्षण	१०३	རང་གི་མཚན་ཉིད
स्वलक्षण	१०३	རང་གི་མཚན་ཉིད་དེ
स्ववचन	१११	རང་གི་ཚིག
स्ववचनैः	१११	རང་གི་ཚིག་རྣམས་ཀྱིས
स्वार्थ	१०४	རང་གི་དོན
स्वार्थ	१०६	བདག་གི་དོན་གྱི
ह ।		
हर्ष	१०६	ཡོང་
हि	१०९	ནི
हेतु	१०६, १०७, ११५	རྒྱུ
हेतु	१०४, १०८, १०९, ११०, ११५	གཏན་ཚིགས
हेतु	११६	གཏན་ཚིགས་ནི
हेतुत्वात्	१०८	གཏན་ཚིགས་ཡིན་པའི་ཕྱིར་དེ
हेतुत्वात्	११३	རྒྱུ་ཡིན་པའི་ཕྱིར་རོ
हेतोः	१०९, ११८	གཏན་ཚིགས་ཀྱི
हेत्वन्तर	१०६	རྒྱུ་གཞན
हेत्वाभास	११२, ११३, ११५	གཏན་ཚིགས་ལྟར་སྣང་བ

TIBETAN WORDS WITH SANSKRIT EQUIVALENTS.

ཀ།

སྐྱེས་བུ	2	पुरुष
སྐྱོན	185, 219, 220	दोष
བསྐལ་བ་ཡིན་པའི་ཕྱིར	172	विप्रकर्षात्
བསྐལ་བའི	62	विप्रकृष्ट
བསྐོར་བ	21	भ्रमण
བསྐྱེད་པའི ...	21	आश्रित
བསྐྱེད་པའི ...	28	जनित

ཁ།

ཁ་ན་མ་ཐོ་བ་མེད་པར ...	138	अवद्य
ཁས་ལེན་དུ་ཟིན ...	127	अभ्युपगमे
ཁས་ལེན་པའི་ཕྱིར་རོ ...	142	अभ्युपगमात्
ཁོ་ན	61, 111, 117, 124, 195 ...	एव
ཁོ་ན་སྟེ	151	एव
ཁོ་ན་དག་ལ ...	86	एव
ཁོ་ན་དང་ལྡན་པ ...	48	एव
ཁོ་ནི་ནི	180	एव
ཁོ་ན་ཡིན་དེ	61	एवेति
ཁོ་ན་ལས	62	एव
ཁོ་ནར	51, 105, 111, 119, 122, 128, 124, 125 ...	एव
ཁོང་དུ་ཆུད་པར་བྱ་སྟེ ...	105	अवगन्तव्याः

ག །

Tibetan	Page	Sanskrit
གང་ཞིག	132, 207, 211 ...	यः
གང་ཞེ་ན	165	कयोः
གང་ཡིན་པ	117	यत्
གང་ཡིན་པ	154	यः
གང་ཡིན་པ	85	ये
གང་ཡིན་པའོ ...	127	यः
གང་ཡོད	122	यः
གང་ལ	129, 174, 213 ...	यत्र
གལ་ཏེ	127	यदि
གལ་ཏེ	213	यद्यपि
གེགས་བྱེད་པའི་ཕྱིར་རོ	219	प्रतिबन्धात्
གོ་བའི་ཕྱིར ...	198	गतत्वात्
གོ་བར་བྱ་བ ...	140	प्रतिपाद्य
གོ་བར་བྱེད་དེ ...	56	गमयेत्
གོ་བར་བྱེད་པ ...	140	प्रतिपादक
གོམས་པ་ལས ...	84	अभ्यासात्
གཽ་ད་མ	210	गौतम
གྱུར་པ	53	भाविन्
གྱུར་པའི	100	भूत
གྲག་པའི	147	आपात
གྲགས་པ	182	प्रतीति
གྲགས་པས ...	134	प्रतीति (inst.)

གྲང་བ	73, 76, 158 ...	शीत
གྲངས་ཅན	144	सांख्य
གྲུ	21	नौ
གྲུབ་སྟེ	97	सिद्ध
གྲུབ་པ	105, 111, 188 ...	सिद्ध
གྲུབ་པ	129, 166 ...	सिद्धि
གྲུབ་པ་ནི	164	सिद्धि
གྲུབ་པ་ལ	108	निष्पत्तौ
གྲུབ་པོ	119	सिद्धि ।
གྲུར་ཞུགས་པ ...	21	नौयान
དགག་པ	55, 62, 82, 85 ...	प्रतिषेध
འགགས་པ ...	142	निरोध
འགའ་ཞིག	97, 209	कश्चित्
འགའ་ཞིག་ན ...	49, 191	क्वचित्
འགའ་ཞིག་ལ ...	127	क्वचित्
འགལ་བ	47, 72, 73, 76, 77 79, 85, 164, 167, 182, 184	विरुद्ध
འགལ་བ	87, 153, 161 ...	विरोध
འགལ་བ་སྟེ ..	155	विरोध
འགལ་བ་དག ...	166	विरुद्धौ
འགལ་བ་ནི	154	विरोध
འགལ་བ་མི་འཁྲུལ་པ་ཅན	182	विरुद्धाव्यभिचारी

འགལ་བ་མི་འཁྲུལ་པ་ཅན་ཉི	185 ...	. विरुद्धाव्यभिचारी
འགལ་བའི	80, 165, 191 ...	विरुद्ध
འགལ་བའོ ...	168	विरुद्ध
འགལ་བས	74	विरुद्ध
འགྱུར	74	भावी
འགྱུར་པས	84, 118	भवति
འགྱུར་བའོ ...	51	भवति
འགྱུར་རོ	82	उपयान्ति
འགྱུར་རོ	119, 121, 122, 128, 130 ...	भवति
འགྲུབ་པ	2, 34, 62, 219 ...	सिद्धि
འགྲུབ་པའི་ཕྱིར ...	34	सिद्धेः
འགྲུབ་པར་བྱེད་པའི་ཕྱིར	102	निष्पत्तौ
འགྲུབ་བོ	61	सिद्धि
རྒོལ་བ	128, 138, 144 ...	वादिन्
རྒོལ་བའི	138	वादिनः
རྒོལ་བས	126	वादिना
རྒྱ་གར	1	[भारत]
རྒྱ་གར་སྐད་དུ ...	1	[भारत भाषायाम्]
རྒྱུ	74, 90	हेतु
རྒྱུ	70, 76, 78, 79, 80, 85, 87, 111, 155, 168	कारण
རྒྱུ་གཞན	74	हेत्वन्तर

Tibetan	Pages	Sanskrit
རྒྱུ་ཡིན་པའི་ཕྱིར་རོ ...	153	हेतुत्वात्
རྒྱུར	182	हेतु (loc.)
རྒྱུ་ལ	93	कारणे
སྒོ	117	मुख
སྒོ་ནས	117	मुखेन
སྒྲ	125, 138, 141, 149	शब्द
སྒྲ་ནི	104, 118, 133, 200, 208, 215	शब्द
སྒྲ་ལ	125	शब्दे
སྒྲུབ་པ	55, 127, 209, 210, 219	साधन
སྒྲུབ་པ་ཁོ་ནར ...	125	साधनत्वेन
སྒྲུབ་པ་ཉིད	125	साधनत्व
སྒྲུབ་པ་ཉིད་དུ ...	138	साधनत्वेन
སྒྲུབ་པ་ལྟར་སྣང་བ ...	140	साधनाभास
སྒྲུབ་པ་པོ	64	प्रतिपत्तृ
སྒྲུབ་པ་ཡིན་པས ...	191	साधनात्
སྒྲུབ་པ་ལ	176	प्रसिद्धे
སྒྲུབ་པ་ལས་ལྡོག་པ་ལ་ཐེ་ཚོམ་ཟ་བ་ནི	209	सन्दिग्धसाधन-व्यतिरेक
སྒྲུབ་པའི	85	साधनी
སྒྲུབ་པའི	105, 185, 193 ...	साधन
སྒྲུབ་པའི་སྐྱོན ...	219	साधनदोष

སྒྲུབ་པའི་ཆོས	...	104	...	...	साधनधर्म्म
སྒྲུབ་པའི་ཕྱིར	...	166, 168		...	साधनात्
སྒྲུབ་པར ...	...	128, 182, 138		...	साधयितुम्
སྒྲུབ་པར་བྱེད་པ	...	200, 212...		...	साधन
སྒྲུབ་པས ...	...	170	...	...	साधन
བརྒྱུད་པའི་སྒོ་ནས	...	82	...	...	पारम्पर्य्येण
བསྒོམས་པ ...	...	27	...	...	भावना
བསྒྲུབ་པ་ལ	...	141, 142, 144, 147, 149, 151, 165			साध्ये
བསྒྲུབ་པར་བྱ་བ	...	116, 124, 166, 181, 200, 201, 206, 207			साध्य
བསྒྲུབ་པར་བྱ་བ	...	58	...	...	साध्यधर्मं
བསྒྲུབ་པར་བྱ་བ་ཁོ་ནར་ནི		125	...	...	साध्यत्वेन
བསྒྲུབ་པར་བྱ་བ་ཉིད་དུ་ནི		170	...	...	साध्यत्वेन
བསྒྲུབ་པར་བྱ་བ་ཡིན་གྱི		128	...	...	साध्य
བསྒྲུབ་པར་བྱ་བ་ཡིན་ཏེ		129, 180		...	साध्य
བསྒྲུབ་པར་བྱ་བ་ཡིན་ན		125	...	...	साध्य
བསྒྲུབ་པར་བྱ་བ་ཡིན་ནོ		188	...	...	साध्य
བསྒྲུབ་པར་བྱ་བ་ལ	...	145	...	...	सिद्धौ
བསྒྲུབ་པར་བྱ་བ་ལས་ལྡོག་པ་ལ་ཐེ་ཚོམ་ཟ་བ		207	...	...	सन्दिग्धसाध्यव्यतिरेक
བསྒྲུབ་པར་བྱ་བའི	...	46, 58, 59, 105, 170			साध्य
བསྒྲུབ་པར་བྱ་བ་ལ	...	111, 115, 125		...	साध्ये
བསྒྲུབ་བྱ ...	...	212	...	...	साध्य

ང་།

དངོས་པོར	163	भाव (loc.)
དངོས་སུ་ན	59	वस्तुनः
དངོས་སུ་ན	107	वस्तुतः
མངོན་པར་འབྲེལ་ཏོ ...	188	अभिसंबध्यते
མངོན་པར་འབྲེལ་བ ...	187	संबध्यते
མངོན་སུམ	2, 13, 33, 37, 40, 51, 62, 64, 90, 182, 183 ...	प्रत्यक्ष
མངོན་སུམ་ནི ...	14	प्रत्यक्ष
མངོན་སུམ་མོ ...	21	प्रत्यक्ष
སྔར	219	पूर्वं
སྔོན་དུ་འགྲོ་བ་ཅན ...	2	पूर्विका
སྔོན་པོ	111	नील

ཅ།

ཅི་ལྟ་བུ	123	कीदृश
ཅི་ཡང	96, 170, 193 ...	कश्चित्
ཅིག་ཅར་དུ ...	187, 188 ...	युगपत्
ཅིག་ཤོས	179	अपर
ཅིག་ཤོས་ནི ...	128	इतर
ཅིག་ཤོས་ལ ...	181	इतरयोः
ཅིག་ཤོས་ལ་ནི ...	171	अपरस्य
ཅིའི་ཕྱིར	169	कस्मात्
ཅེས་བྱ་བ་ནི ...	126	इति

ཆོས་མི་མཐུན་པའི ...	207, 209 ...	वैधर्म्यं
ཆོས་མི་མཐུན་པའི་དཔེ་ནི	209	वैधर्म्योदाहरण
ཆོས་མི་མཐུན་པས ...	115, 206 ...	वैधर्म्येण
ཆོས་སུ	149	धर्मे
འཆི་བ་ནི	142	मरण
འཆི་བ་ཡིན་པར ...	142	मरण

ཇ།

ཇི་སྐད་སྨོས་པ ...	62	यथोक्त
ཇི་སྐད་སྨོས་པའི ...	195	यथोक्त
ཇི་ལྟ་བ་དེ་བཞིན་དུ་གནས་པར	186	यथावस्थित
ཇི་ལྟ་བུ་དག་གིས ...	105	यथा
ཇི་རིགས་པར ...	182	यथायोगं
འཇིག་པ་ནི	74	विनाश
འཇུག་སྟེ	64	साधनी
རྗེས་སུ་འགྲོ་བ ...	177	अन्वेति
རྗེས་སུ་འགྲོ་བ ...	115, 117, 119, 171, 178, 179, 202, 204 ...	अन्वय
རྗེས་སུ་འགྲོ་བ་ཕྱིན་ཅི་ལོག་ནི	204	विपरीतान्वय
རྗེས་སུ་འགྲོ་བ་མེད་པ ...	202	अनन्वय
རྗེས་སུ་འགྲོ་བ་རབ་ཏུ་མ་སྟན་པ་ནི	202	अप्रदर्शितान्वय

ཉ།

ཉི་མས	... ...	221	[रवि]
ཉིད	... ...	30, 33, 41, 43, 128, 138, 151, 154	एव
ཉིད་ཀྱི་ཕྱིར་རོ	...	79	त्वात्
ཉིད་ཀྱིས	... ...	158	त्वेन
ཉིད་དུ	... ...	44, 141	एव
ཉིད་ལ	... ...	114, 194, 217 ...	एव
ཉེ་བ	... ...	80	सन्निधान
ཉེ་བ	... ...	79	संनिहित
ཉེ་བར་སྟོན་པའོ	...	104	उपदर्शन
ཉེས་པ་རྣམས	...	199	दोषाः
གཉི་ག	... ...	218	उभय
གཉི་ག་ལ	... ...	120	द्वयोः
གཉི་ག་ལ་མ་གྲུབ་པ	...	141	उभयासिद्ध
གཉི་ག་ལས་ལྡོག་པ	...	211	उभयव्यतिरेक
གཉི་ག་ལས་ལྡོག་པ་ལ་ཐེ་ཚོམ་ཟ་བ་ནི		211	सन्दिग्धोभय-व्यतिरेक
གཉིས	... ...	164, 207 ...	द्वि
གཉིས་ཀ	... ...	140, 200 ...	उभय
གཉིས་ཀྱིས	... ...	118	द्वय
གཉིས་གཉིས་ལ	...	182	द्वयोर्द्वयोः

གཉིས་དེ	117	द्वि
གཉིས་སྟེ	12	द्वि
གཉིས་ནི	55	द्वौ
གཉིས་པ	165	द्वि
གཉིས་པ	190	द्वितीय
གཉིས་པ་ནི	38	द्वितीय
གཉིས་པའི	91	द्वितीय
གཉིས་ལས	171	द्वयोः
མཉན་དུ་མི་རུང་ངོ	188	अश्रावणा

ད།

གཏན་ཚིགས	58, 55, 99, 110, 114, 116, 125, 198	हेतु
གཏན་ཚིགས་ཀྱི	115, 217	हेतोः
གཏན་ཚིགས་ལྟར་སྣང་བ	141, 149, 165, 182	हेत्वाभास
གཏན་ཚིགས་ནི	194	हेतु
གཏན་ཚིགས་ཡིན་པའི་ཕྱིར་དེ	107	हेतुत्वात्
གཏན་ཚིགས་སུ	111	हेतु (loc.)
བཏགས་པའི་ཕྱིར་རོ	93	उपचारात्
རྟག་པ	200, 216	नित्य
རྟག་པ་ཉིད	149, 165	नित्यत्व
རྟག་པའི	183	नित्य

རྟགས ...	...	39, 48, 58, 92, 118, 139	...	लिङ्ग
རྟགས་ནི ...	...	41, 195 ...	...	लिङ्ग
རྟགས་སུ་གྱུར་པ	...	207 ...	...	लिङ्गभूत
རྟོག་པ ...	...	14 ...	...	कल्पना
རྟོག་པ་དང་བྲལ་ཞིང་	...	14 ...	...	कल्पनापोढ
རྟོག་པ་ནི ...	...	17 ...	...	कल्पना
རྟོགས་དེ ...	...	114, 115	...	गति
རྟོགས་པ ...	...	162 ...	...	गति
རྟོགས་པ ...	...	38, 34 ...	...	प्रतीति
རྟོགས་པའི་ཕྱིར	...	119 ...	...	प्रतीतेः
རྟོགས་པར ...	...	84 ...	...	प्रतीति (loc.)
རྟོགས་པས ...	...	193 ...	...	प्रतीति
ལྟ་བར་བྱའོ	...	108 ...	...	द्रष्टव्याः
ལྟ་བུ་སྟེ ...	...	210, 212	...	इति
ལྟ་བུའོ ...	...	158 ...	...	वत्
ལྟ་བུའོ་ཞེས	...	195 ...	...	इति
ལྟ་བུའོ་ཞེས་བྱ་བ་ནི	...	100 ...	...	इति
ལྟག་གཅོད་རྣམས	...	220 ...	...	ज्ञात्यन्तराणि
ལྟག་གཅོད་རྣམས	...	220 ...	...	ज्ञातयः
སྟན ...	...	130, 167	...	आसन
སྟོན་པ ...	...	186 ...	...	उपसंहार

བསྟན་པར ...	... 118	... ...	ख्यापन (loc.)
བསྟན་པར ...	... 120	... ...	निर्देश (loc.)
བསྟན་པར ...	... 138	... ...	दर्शित (loc.)
བསྟན་པར་བྱ་བར	... 195	... ...	दर्शनीयौ
བསྟན་པར་བྱ་ཞིན	... 123	... ...	निर्देश्य
བསྟན་པར་བྱའོ	... 117	... ...	दर्शनीय
བསྟན་པས ...	... 122	... ...	उक्ते

ཐ །

ཐ་སྙད ...	... 64, 85, 97, 121, 122	...	व्यवहार
ཐ་དད ...	... 82	... ...	भेद
ཐ་དད་པ ...	... 80	... ...	भेद
ཐ་དད་པ ...	... 170	... ...	भिद्यते (भिन्न)
ཐ་དད་པ་ཅན་ཉིད	... 103	... ...	भेदित्व
ཐམས་ཅད ...	... 2, 25, 99. 142, 175, 188, 218		सर्व
ཐམས་ཅད་ཀྱི	... 117	... ...	सर्वस्य
ཐམས་ཅད་མཁྱེན་པ	... 151, 152, 154, 171, 172, 207		सर्वज्ञ
ཐམས་ཅད་མཁྱེན་པ་ཉིད	158, 161	...	सर्वज्ञत्व
ཐམས་ཅད་མཁྱེན་པ་མ ...	201	... ...	असर्वज्ञ
ཐམས་ཅད་མཁྱེན་པ་མ་ཡིན་པ	153	... ...	असर्वज्ञ
ཐམས་ཅད་ན	... 187	... ...	सर्व (loc.)

Tibetan	Pages	Sanskrit
ཐེ་ཚོམ་ཟ་བའི་ཕྱིར་རོ་	154	सन्देहात्
ཐོགས་པ་མེད་པ	70, 76	अप्रतिबद्ध
མཐའ	27	पर्यन्त
མཐའ་ལས་བྱུང་བའི	27	पर्यन्तज
མཐུན་པ	46	समान
མཐུན་པའི་ཕྱོགས	43, 47, 118, 149, 194, 195, 217	सपक्ष
མཐུན་པའི་ཕྱོགས་ནི	46	सपक्ष
མཐུན་པའི་ཕྱོགས་ལ	165, 166	सपक्षे
མཐོང་བ	84	दर्शन
མཐོང་བ	97	दृष्ट
མཐོང་བའི	185	दर्शन (gen.)

ད།

Tibetan	Pages	Sanskrit
ད་ལྟར	64	वर्त्तमान
དག་གིས	82	भ्यां
དག་པ	100	शुद्ध
དང་	13, 23, 39, 41, 47, 48, 51, 59, 60, 64, 86, 106, 108, 202	च
དང་ལྡན་པའི	81	युक्त
དང་པོ་ནི	2	प्रथम
དང་པོ་འདི	37	प्रथम
དམ	218	च

དམ	145, 172, 218	वा
དུ་བ	69, 70, 78, 110, 114, 195	धूम
དུ་བ་ཡོད	110	धूम
དུ་བ་ཡོད་པའི་ཕྱིར	54, 73, 81	धूमात्
དུམ་བུ	218	खण्ड
དུས	62	काल
དེ	132	एतत्
དེ	58, 117, 128, 154, 169, 182	सः
དེ	2, 30, 33, 62, 99, 108, 115, 116, 117, 125, 127, 129, 138, 147, 195	तद्
དེ་ཉིད	30, 33, 106	तदेव
དེ་ཉིད་ཀྱི་ཕྱིར	179	अतएव
དེ་ཉིད་ཀྱིས	68	तस्या एव
དེ་གཉིས	61	ते
དེ་གཉིས་ཁོ་ནས	61	ताभ्यामेव
དེ་གཉིས་དང	176	ताभ्यां
དེ་གཉིས་ནི	166	एतौ
དེ་གཉིས་ལ	172	द्वयोः
དེ་ལྟ་བས་ན	117, 185	तस्मात्
དེ་ལྟ་བུ	119	तादृश
དེ་ལྟར	112, 182	एवं

Tibetan		References	Sanskrit
དེ་ལྟར་ན	... ...	118, 138, 164 ...	इति
དེ་དག	... ...	219	ते
དེ་དག	... ...	82	इमे
དེ་དག	... ...	104, 218	एते
དེ་དག	... ...	107	तयोः
དེ་དག་གིས ...	...	217	एभिः
དེ་དག་ཐམས་ཅད་ལ	...	85	सर्वत्र
དེ་དག་ཉི	... ...	85	ते
དེ་དང	... ...	57, 188	तद्
དེ་དང་	... ...	21	तया
དེ་དང་	... ...	60	तत्र
དེ་དང་འགལ་བ	...	47	तद्विरुद्ध
དེ་དྲ་བའི	... ...	122	तादृश
དེ་ན	... ...	54	अत्र
དེ་ན	... ...	110, 190, 195 ...	तत्र
དེ་ནི	... ...	122	तथा
དེ་ནི	... ...	170	अयं
དེ་ནི	... ...	68	सा
དེ་ནི	... ...	142	अनेन (nom.)
དེ་ནི	... ...	82, 197, 121, 122 ... 129, 132, 189, 202. 218	सः

དེའི་ཕྱིར	218	तद् (ablat.)
དེའི་ཚེ	127, 128, 138 ...	तदा
དེའི་རང་བཞིན་མ་ཡིན་པ	60	अतत्स्वभाव
དེར	57	तद् (loc.)
དེས	117, 128, 219 ...	तेन
དེས་ན	130	अनेन
དེས་ན	127	एतेन
དེས་ན	193	तेन
དོན	2, 27, 30, 31, 33, ... 34, 46, 59, 82, 90, 129, 130, 132, 135, 191, 193, 195, 219	अर्थ
དོན་གྱི་དབང་གིས ...	218	अर्थापत्त्या
དོན་གྱིས	56	अर्थ (instr.)
དོན་གྱིས་ནི	114	अर्थात्
དོན་དམ་པ	30	परमार्थ
དོན་དམ་པར་ཡོད་པ ...	30	परमार्थसत्
དོན་དུ་ནི	96	अर्थतः
དོན་རྣམས་ལ ...	186	अर्थेषु
དོན་བྱེད	31	अर्थक्रिया
དོན་བྱེད་ནུས་པ་ཁོ་ན ...	31	अर्थक्रियासामर्थ्य
དོན་དམིགས་པའི་རིག་བྱར་མ་གྱུར་པ་རྣམས་ལ	62	अनुपलब्धि-लक्षणप्राप्तेषु

Tibetan	Page	Sanskrit
བདག་མེད་པ་ལས	178	निरात्मकात्
བདག་མེད་པར	176	निरात्मकत्वेन
བདུད	221	[मार]
བདེ་བ	144	सुख
འདས་པ	64	अतीत
འདི	120, 191, 195	अयं
འདི་གཉིས	170	आभ्यां (nom.)
འདི་གཉིས	96	अनयोः (nom.)
འདི་གཉིས་ཁོ་ནའི	169	अनयोरेव
འདི་གཉིས་ནི	166	अनयोः (nom.)
འདི་གཉིས་ལས	175	अनयोः
འདི་ན	69, 71, 72, 73, 77, 78, 121, 122	अत्र
འདི་ན	79	अस्य
འདི་ན	70, 76, 110, 112, 121, 146	इह
འདི་ན་ནི	114	अत्र
འདི་ནི	53, 81, 201	अयं
འདི་ལ	55	अत्र
འདི་ལ་ནི	171	अत्र
འདིར	121	अस्मात्
འདིར	187	तत्र
འདིར	111, 122, 182	इह

འདོད་པ	138	अभिमत
འདོད་པ	123, 128, 129, 138, 170	इष्ट
འདོད་པ་ཡིན་གྱི	125	इष्ट
འདོད་པ་ལ་གནོད་པ་བྱེད་པའི་ཕྱིར	167	इष्टविघातकृत्
འདོད་པའི	132, 202, 219	इष्ट
འདོད་པའོ	124	इष्ट
འདོད་པས	129	इष्टता
འདྲ་བ་ཉིད	34	सारूप्य
འདྲའོ	40	वत्
འདྲེ	17	संसर्ग
འདྲེར་རུང	17	संसर्गयोग्य
རྡུལ་ཕྲ་རབ	200, 206	परमाणु
རྡོ	213	उपल
རྡོའི་དུམ་བུ	213	उपलखण्ड
ལྡན་པ	201, 202, 210	मान्
ལྡན་པ་སྟེ	210	मन्तः
ལྡན་པའི་ཕྱིར	211	योगात्
ལྡན་པའི་ཕྱིར	201	मत्त्वात्
ལྡན་པའི་ཕྱིར་རོ	209	मत्त्वात्
ལྡོག་པ	164, 207, 209, 212, 214, 215	व्यतिरेक

ལྡོག་པ	116, 117	निवृत्ति
ལྡོག་པ་ཉིད་དུ	176	व्यावृत्तत्वेन
ལྡོག་པ་གཉིས	178	व्यतिरेकयोः (nom.)
ལྡོག་པ་གཉིས་ནི	179	व्यतिरेकयोः (nom.)
ལྡོག་པ་གཉིས་ལ	179	व्यतिरेकयोः
ལྡོག་པ་ནི	158	व्यावृत्ति
ལྡོག་པ་ནི	168	विवृत्ति
ལྡོག་པ་ནི	154, 171	व्यतिरेक
ལྡོག་པ་ལ	151	व्यावृत्तिक
ལྡོག་པ་ལས	158	विपर्ययात्
ལྡོག་པ་ཕྱིན་ཅི་ལོག་ནི	216	विपरीतव्यतिरेक
ལྡོག་པ་མེད་པ	214	अव्यतिरेक
ལྡོག་པ་རབ་ཏུ་མ་བསྟན་པ་ནི	215	अप्रदर्शितव्यतिरेक
ལྡོག་པ་མེད་པ་ནི	213	अव्यतिरेक
ལྡོག་པ་ཡོད་མེད་ཀྱི	213	व्यावृत्तया
ལྡོག་པའི	194	व्यावृत्त
ལྡོག་པའི	117	व्यतिरेक
ལྡོག་པའི་སྒོ་ནས	117	व्यतिरेकमुखेन
སྡེ་བོ	221	[सेना]
སྡོང་རིས	207	वर्धमान
བསྡུས་པ	117	आक्षिप्त
བསྡུས་པའི་ཕྱིར་རོ	175	संग्रहात्

11

ན།

ནང་དུ་འདུས་པའི་ཕྱིར་རོ	169	अन्तर्भावात्
ནམ	144	वा
ནམ་མཁའ	187, 195, 206, 215...	आकाश
ནི	117	हि
ནུས་དེ	218	शक्य
ནུས་པ	70, 76	सामर्थ्यं
ནུས་པ་ཁོ་ན... ...	31	सामर्थ्यं
ནུས་སོ	195	शक्य
ནཱམ	1	[नाम]
ནྱཱ་ཡ་བི་ནྡུ	1	[न्यायबिन्दु]
གནས་པ	187	अवस्थित
གནས་པ	187	गत
གནས་པ	175	वृत्ति
གནས་པའི	158	स्थित
གནས་པར	175	वृत्ति
གནས་པར	188	अवस्थित
གནས་པར་འགྱུར་བ ...	174	वर्त्तते
རྣམ་པ	68, 117	प्रकार
རྣམ་པ	12, 28	विधा

པ།

དཔེར་ན	...	48, 53, 54, 69, 70-74, 76-80, 97, 99, 110, 111, 125, 130, 133, 135, 141, 145-147, 149, 151, 167, 171, 173, 200, etc. ...	यथा
དཔྱད་པ་དག་ལ	...	185 ...	विचारेषु
སྤངས་ཏེ	...	158 ...	परिहार
སྤུ	...	79, 81 ...	रोम
སྤུ་ལོང	...	79, 81 ...	रोमहर्ष
སྤྱི	...	187, 191, 217 ...	सामान्य
སྤྱི་དང	...	46 ...	सामान्येन
སྤྱིའི	...	82 ...	सामान्य
སྤྱིའི་མཚན་ཉིད	...	217 ...	सामान्यलक्षण

ཕ།

ཕ་རོལ་པོ	...	219 ...	पर
ཕན་ཚུན	...	191 ...	परस्पर
ཕན་ཚུན	...	179 ...	अन्योन्य
ཕུང་པོ	...	174 ...	राशि
ཕྱལ་དུ་ཕྱིན་པ	...	207 ...	अतिप्लव
ཕྱི་རྒོལ་བ	...	142 ...	प्रतिवादि
ཕྱིན་ཅི་ལོག	...	164, 166, 168 ...	विपर्यय
ཕྱིན་ཅི་ལོག་ཏེ	...	204 ...	विपरीत

བྱེ་བྲག ...	... 96, 108 ...	... भेद
བྱེ་བྲག ...	... 48, 79, 81, 84, 97, 112, 170 ...	... विशेष
བྱེ་བྲག་གི ...	... 218 ...	... विशेष
བྱེ་བྲག་གི་མཚན་ཉིད ...	218 ...	... विशेषलक्षण
བྱེ་བྲག་གིས ...	... 100 ...	... भेदेन
བྱེ་བྲག་གིས ...	... 68, 94 ...	... भेदात्
བྱེད་བྲག་གིས་དེ ...	101 ...	... भेदेन
བྱེ་བྲག་ཏུ་ནི ...	... 194 ...	... विशेषेण
བྱེ་བྲག་དག ...	... 79 ...	... विशेषाः
བྱེ་བྲག་དང་ལྡན་པའི ...	45 ...	... विशेष
བྱེ་བྲག་མེད་པར ...	194 ...	... अभेदेन
བྱེད ...	... 81 ...	... क्रिया
བྱེད་པ ...	... 210 ...	... प्रयोक्तृ
བྱེད་པ ...	... 102 ...	... व्यापार
བྱེད་པས ...	... 127 ...	... कारेण
བྲམ་ཟེ་ནི ...	... 209 ...	... ब्राह्मण
བྲལ་བ ...	... 211, 218 ...	... वीत
བྲལ་བ་ཉིད ...	... 212 ...	... वीतत्व
བྲལ་བ་མ ...	... 211, 218 ...	... अवीत
བྲལ་བའི ...	... 207 ...	... अविद्यमान
བྲལ་བའོ ...	... 176 ...	व्यतिरिच्यते

སྦྱོར་བ	68, 82, 84, 94, 96, ... 99, 118, 120, 189, 190	प्रयोग
སྦྱོར་བ་ནི	110, 111... ...	प्रयोग
སྦྱོར་བ་ལ	114, 121, 122 ...	प्रयोगे
སྦྱོར་བའོ	100, 112, 118, 114...	प्रयोग

མ།

མ	185	अ
མ	97, 158, 169, 176, ... 182, 198	न
མ་བསྐྱེད་པའི ...	21	अनाहित
མ་འཁྲུལ་བ ...	14	अभ्रान्त
མ་གྲུབ	138	असिद्ध
མ་གྲུབ་སྟེ	142	असिद्ध
མ་གྲུབ་ན	108	अनिष्पन्नस्य
མ་གྲུབ་ན	147, 148	असिद्धौ
མ་གྲུབ་པ	147, 182... ...	असिद्ध
མ་གྲུབ་པ	171, 182... ...	असिद्धि
མ་གྲུབ་པ་ཡིན་ཏེ ...	145	असिद्ध
མ་གྲུབ་པའི... ...	141	असिद्ध
མ་གྲུབ་པའི་ཕྱིར ...	125	असिद्धत्वात्
མ་གྲུབ་པའི་ཕྱིར ...	176, 177, 214 ...	असिद्धेः
མ་གྲུབ་པའི་ཕྱིར་རོ ...	168	असिद्धेः

མ་ཡིན་ནོ	81, 128, 132, 135, ... 152, 162, 170, 189	न
མ་ཡིན་པ	151, 168, 207 ...	न
མ་ཡིན་པའི	220	अभूत
མ་ལུས་པ	221	[अघोष]
མ་བསལ་བ	182	अनिराकृत
མ་བསལ་བ་ནི ...	188	अनिराकृत
མ་བསལ་བས ...	123	अनिराकृत
མང་ཞིག	127	अनेक
མལ་ཆ	130, 167	प्रायन
མི	151, 201, 209 ...	पुरुष
མི	112, 114, 121, 122, ... 125, 154, 184, 187, 190, 191, 195, 202, 209, 210, 218	न
མི་འཁྲུལ་པ་ཅན ...	184	अव्यभिचारी
མི་འཁྲུལ་པར ...	57	अव्यभिचार
མི་འགལ་བ	162	अविरुद्ध
མི་འགྲུབ་པའི་ཕྱིར་རོ ...	87, 90, 116 ...	असिद्धेः
མི་ཉེ་བ་དག	80	असन्निधान
མི་རྟག་པ	141, 203, 204, 215 ...	अनित्य
མི་རྟག་པ་ཉིད ...	113, 195	अनित्यत्व
མི་རྟག་པ་ཉིད་དུ ...	125	अनित्यत्वे
མི་རྟག་པ་ཉིད་ནི ...	144	अनित्यत्व

མི་དམིགས་པས	85	अनुपलब्धा
མི་རྨོངས་པར	64	अमूढ़
མི་སྲིད་དེ	195	असम्भव
མི་སྲིད་པའི་ཕྱིར	161	असम्भवात्
མི་སྲིད་པའི་ཕྱིར་རོ	62, 183	असंभवात्
མིག	130, 167	चक्षुः
མིག་གིས་གཟུང་བ་ཉིད་ནི	125, 141	चाक्षुषत्व
མུ་སྟེགས	221	[तीर्थिक]
མེ	54, 78, 114, 145, 195	अग्नि
མེ་ཡོང་དེ	110	अग्नि
མེ་ཡོད་པའི་ཕྱིར	73, 76, 77	अग्नेः
མེད	172	असत्त्व
མེད་དེ	190	नास्ति
མེད་དེ	49, 69, 70, 74, 79, 175, 178, 195, 212	न
མེད་དོ	191	अविद्यमान
མེད་དོ	71, 73, 77, 78, 96, 118, 119, 121, 122, 170, 174, 177, 184, 193	न
མེད་ན	213	नास्ति
མེད་ན	116, 195	अभावे
མེད་ན	113, 114, 195	असति
མེད་ན་ནི	115, 116	असति

དམིགས་པ་འགྱུར་ན	...	122	... ...	उपलभ्यते
དམིགས་པ་ནི	...	72, 73, 74, 76, 77, 79, 80	...	उपलब्धि
དམིགས་པའི	...	147	... ...	उपलभमान
དམིགས་པར་འགྱུར་ཏེ	...	111	... ...	उपलभ्यते
དམིགས་སོ ...	...	112	... ...	उपलब्धि
དམིགས་སོ ...	...	97, 121, 122, 191	...	उपलभ्यते
མ་བྱ ...	...	146	... ...	मयूर
མ་བྱའི་སྒྲ་སྒྲོག་པའི་ཕྱིར		146	... ...	केकायितात्
སྨྲོས་ཏེ ...	...	182	... ...	उक्त
སྨྲོས་པ ...	...	184, 193, 219	...	उक्त
སྨྲོས་པ་ཡིན་ནོ	...	117	... ...	उक्त
སྨྲ་བ ...	...	151, 152, 153, 154, 202, 213	...	वक्तृ
སྨྲ་བ་ཉིད ...	...	153, 161...	...	वक्तृत्व
སྨྲ་བའི་ཕྱིར...	...	171, 218...	...	वक्तृत्वात्
སྨྲ་བའི་ཕྱིར་ན	...	201	... ...	वक्तृत्वात्
སྨྲས ...	...	140	.. ...	उक्तौ
སྨྲས་ན ...	...	127	... ...	आह
སྨྲས་ན ...	...	140	... ...	उक्तौ
སྨྲས་པ ...	...	127	... ...	आह
སྨྲས་པ ...	...	170	... ...	उक्त
སྨྲས་པ་ནི ...	...	219	... ...	उक्ति

ཚུལ	... ...	39, 48, 92, 139, 141, 148, 151, 164, 171, 172, 182	... रूप
ཚུལ་ནི	... ...	195	... ... रूप
ཚུལ་གསུམ་པ	...	39, 92	... ... त्रिरूप
ཚུལ་གསུམ་པ་ཉིད	...	41	... ... त्रैरूप्य
ཚུལ་གསུམ་པའི	...	139	... ... त्रिरूप
ཚུལ་གསུམ་པོ	...	48	... ... त्रिरूप
ཚེ	... ...	142	... ... आयुः
མཚན་ཉིད	... ...	193	... ... रूप
མཚན་ཉིད	... ...	82, 132, 138, 142, ... 184, 193, 217, ... 218	लक्षण
མཚན་ཉིད་ཁོ་ན་སྟེ	...	158	... ... लक्षणता
མཚན་ཉིད་དེ	...	28	... ... लक्षण
མཚན་ཉིད་ནི	...	31, 90	... ... लक्षण
མཚུངས་པ་དེ་མ་ཐག་པ		23	... ... समनन्तर

ཛ།

རྫོགས་སོ	... ...	221	... ... समाप्त

ཞ།

ཞུགས་པ	... ...	21	... ... यान
ཞུགས་པ་ཡིན་པས་ན	...	185	... ... प्रसक्त

Tibetan	Page	Sanskrit
གཞན	116	अपर
གཞན་གྱི	102	पर
གཞན་གྱི་དོན	39	परार्थ
གཞན་གྱི་དོན་གྱི་རྗེས་སུ་དཔག་པ	92	[परार्थानुमान]
གཞན་གྱི་དོན་གྱི་རྗེས་སུ་དཔག་པ་ནི	92, 139	परार्थानुमान
གཞན་གྱི་དོན་བྱེད་དེ	130, 167	परार्थ
གཞན་གྱི་བྱེད་པ་ལ་བལྟོས་པའི	102	अपेक्षितपरव्यापार
གཞན་གྱི་དོན་བྱེད་པར	168	पारार्थ्य
གཞན་དག་ལ་ནི	87	अन्येषाम्
གཞན་དུ་ན	62, 195	अन्यथा
གཞན་ནི	82, 104, 184	अन्य
གཞན་པ	195	इतर
གཞན་པ	47	अन्य
གཞན་ཡོད་ན	155	अन्यभाव
གཞལ་བྱ་ཉིད	149	प्रमेयत्व
གཞི་ཡིན་པའི་ཕྱིར་རོ	129	अधिकरणत्वात्
གཞི་ལ	145	आश्रयणास्य
བཞི	137	चत्वारः
གཞི་སྡེ	23	चतुर्
བཞིན་དེ	97, 110	तथा

Tibetan	Pages	Sanskrit
ཡང་དག་པའི	27	भूत
ཡང་དག་པའི	2, 12	सम्यक्
ཡང་དག་པའི་དོན	27	भूतार्थ
ཡང་ནི	48	च
ཡན་ལག	130	अङ्ग
ཡན་ལག་ནི	193	अवयव
ཡན་ལག་བཞིན་ནོ	167	अङ्गवत्
ཡིད	23	मनः
ཡིད་ཀྱི་རྣམ་པར་ཤེས་པ	23	मनोविज्ञान
ཡིད་ཆེས་པ་མ	207	अनाप्त
ཡིད་ཆེས་པ་མ་ཡིན་པ	207	अनाप्तता
ཡིན་ཏེ	195	भवति
ཡིན་ཏེ	199	भवन्ति
ཡིན་ནོ	153	उपलभ्यते
ཡིན་ནོ	137	भवन्ति
ཡིན་ནོ	138, 154, 216	भवति
ཡིན་པའི་ཕྱིར	31, 33 53,	त्वात्
ཡིན་པའི་ཕྱིར་རོ	60	त्वात्
ཡིན་པས་ན	2	इति
ཡིན་ལ	117	भवति
ཡུལ	62, 147, 187, 188, 189	देश

ར།

Tibetan	Pages	Sanskrit
རང་	25, 62	आत्मन्
རང་	23, 28, 53	स्व
རང་གི	102, 104, 132	स्व
རང་གི་ངོ་བོ	123, 124	स्वरूप
རང་གི་དོན	39	स्वार्थ
རང་གི་དོན་གྱི་རྗེས་སུ་དཔག་པ	38, 91	[स्वार्थानुमान]
རང་གི་ཚད་མ་ཇི་ལྟ་བུ་དག་གིས	104	यथा स्वं प्रमाणैः
རང་གི་ཚིག	135	स्ववचन
རང་གི་ཚིག་རྣམས་ཀྱིས	132	स्ववचनैः
རང་གི་མཚན་ཉིད	30	स्वलक्षण
རང་གི་མཚན་ཉིད་དེ	28	स्वलक्षण
རང་དང་	187	स्व
རང་བཞིན	48, 51, 56, 60, 61, 62, 69, 72, 82, 85, 99, 100, 113, 116, 184, 186, 188, 191, 195	स्वभाव
རང་བཞིན་གྱི་གཏན་ཚིགས	189	स्वभावहेतु
རང་བཞིན་གྱིས	195	स्वभावेन
རང་བཞིན་ཉིད	189	स्वभावता

རུང་ ...	...	17 ...	... योग्य
རེ་རེ ...	...	182 ...	... एकैकस्य
རེག་པ ...	...	73, 77, 158	... स्पर्श
རྭ ...	...	97 ...	... विषाण
རླངས་པ ...	...	145 ...	... बाष्प

ལ།

ལ་ལ་ཞིག ...	...	151 ...	... कश्चित्
ལ་སོགས་པ...	...	207 ...	... आदिक
ལ་སོགས་པ	...	82, 85, 97, 100, 108, 110, 144, 158, 163, 164, 172, 174, 176, 201, 202, 206, 209, 210, 212, 219	... आदि
ལ་སོགས་པ་དང་ལྡན་པའི		173 ...	... आदिमत्
ལ་སོགས་པ་ནི	...	180, 167, 176, 207, 211	... आदि
ལ་སོགས་པའི	...	151 ...	... आदिक
ལ་སོགས་པའི	...	111, 130, 116, 149, 167	... आदि
ལ་སོགས་པས	...	21 ...	... आदि
ལམ་པོ་ཆེ ...	...	201 ...	... रथ्या
ལས ...	...	200, 206	... कर्म
ལུང་ ...	...	185 ...	... आगम

ཤུགས་ཉིད་ཀྱིས ... 122 ... ... सामर्थ्यात्

ཤུན་པ ... ... 142 ... ... त्वक्

ཤེས་པ ... ... 17 ... ... प्रतीति

ཤེས་པ ... ... 23, 27, 30, 33, 39, 207 ... ज्ञान

ཤེས་པ་ནི ... ... 2, 12, 21 ... ज्ञान

ཤེས་པར་འདོད་པའི ... 45 ... ... जिज्ञासित

བཤད་དེ ... ... 195 ... ... उक्तौ

བཤད་དོ ... ... 185 ... ... उक्त

བཤད་ན ... ... 182 ... ... उक्त

བཤད་པ ... ... 85 ... ... उक्त

བཤད་པ་ལ ... ... 194 ... ... उक्त

བཤད་པར་བྱའོ ... 195 ... ... दर्शनीयम्

བཤུས་ན ... ... 142 ... ... अपहरणे

ས།

སུན་འབྱིན་པ ... 219 ... ... दूषण

སུན་འབྱིན་པ་ལྟར་སྣང་བ་
དག་ནི ... ... 220 ... ... दूषणाभासाः

སུན་འབྱིན་པ་དག ... 219 ... ... दूषणाः

སེམས ... ... 25 ... ... चित्त

སེམས་པ་མེད་པར ... 144 ... ... अचेतनाः

ཧ།